LA BOHÈME

Giacomo Puccini

1858 - 1924

Mimi . . . . Mirella Freni
Rodolfo . . . . Nicolai Gedda
Marcello . . . . Mario Sereni
Schaunard . . . . Mario Basiola, Jr.
Colline . . . . Ferruccio Mazzoli
Musetta . . . . Mariella Adani
Benoit . . . . Carlo Badioli
Alcindoro . . . . Paolo Montarsolo
Parpignol . . . . Vittorio Pandano
Un Doganière . . . . Giuseppe Giuliano
Un Venditore . . . . Antonio Dellaca

Conducted by Thomas Schippers
Orchestra e Coro del Teatro dell'Opera di Roma
Chorus Master: Gianni Lazzari

La Bohème

LA BOHÈME

Giacomo Puccini

TEXT BY DAVID FOIL

Additional commentary by William Berger

BLACK DOG
& LEVENTHAL
PUBLISHERS
NEW YORK

Published by
Black Dog & Leventhal Publishers, Inc.
151 West 19th Street
New York, NY 10011

Distributed by
Workman Publishing Company
708 Broadway
New York, NY 10003

Manufactured in China

Cover and interior design by Liz Driesbach.

Cover image © The Art Archive / Puccini House Torre del Lago / Dagli Orti (A)

ISBN-10 : 1-57912-509-3
ISBN-13 : 978-1-57912-509-7

h g f e d c

Library of Congress Cataloging-in-Publication Data available on file.

*T*here is no better place to begin exploring opera than with *La Bohème*. It tells an irresistible story that is charming, sexy, and, ultimately, heartrending. The action is breathtaking. And, from the opening bars, Puccini's music is unforgettable in its infectious energy, its expressive beauty, and its wealth of melody. It is an experience to cherish, to relive again and again.

You will hear the entire opera on the two compact discs included on the inside front and back covers of this book. As you explore the book, you will discover the story behind the opera and its creation, the background of the composer, biographies of the principal singers and conductor, and the opera's text, or libretto, both in the original Italian and in an English translation. Special commentary has been included throughout the libretto to aid in your appreciation and to highlight key moments in the action and the score.

Enjoy this book and enjoy the music.

La Bohème

*I*n the hundred years since its premiere, Giacomo Puccini's *La Bohème* has become the most consistently popular opera of the twentieth century. It might even be argued that *La Bohème* is the opera that defines opera for modern audiences. That hardly seemed possible the morning after its first performance.

The eagerly awaited premiere of *La Bohème* took place in Turin's Teatro Regio on February 1, 1896, with Arturo Toscanini conducting. Nothing less than a blockbuster was expected

Left: A heartbroken Placido Domingo as Rodolfo clutches Mimì's bonnet.
Above: Giacomo Puccini (1858–1924)

from the promising composer whose opera *Manon Lescaut* had premiered exactly three years earlier, to the day, in the same theater. The first performance of *La Bohème* actually went rather well, with its handpicked cast performing up to the exacting standards that were the hallmarks of any Toscanini performance. The audience seemed to like at least parts of what it was seeing and hearing. Yet there was nothing infectious about its response—in short, no buzz—and a vague sense of disappointment materialized, like a hangover, when the performance ended. The intermission chatter, most of the next morning's reviews, the gossip that would quickly spread through Italy's musical circles—none of it was encouraging.

Most of the critics found *La Bohème* to be inconsequential, vulgar, and lightweight, and unlikely to hold the interest of audiences even through the current season. Carlo Bersenzio typified the critics's reaction with his conclusion in *La stampa*, writing that "*Bohème*, just as it makes little impression on the emotions of the listener, will leave few traces in the history of our lyric theater." That dismissive tone would be echoed by critics at the opera's premieres in London in 1897 and New

York in 1900. That once consummate crank among New York music critics, Henry Krehbiel, began his review of the Metropolitan Opera's premiere of the opera by saying, "*La Bohème* is foul in subject, and fulminant but futile in its music." The apathy of these reactions devastated Puccini, despite the fitful bursts of appreciation from that first audience and Toscanini's passionate assurances that the opera would prevail.

In the midst of all this soul-killing blather, though, something else was happening. *La Bohème* was developing into the best kind of hit there is—a word-of-mouth hit—one that, as a Hollywood observer later said of a smash movie hated by critics and industry insiders, "nobody liked much except the

La Bohème is set in the Paris of Victor Hugo and Honoré de Balzac.

people in the audience." As a matter of fact, *La Bohème* played twenty-four additional performances in Turin to sold-out houses during the remainder of the month of February 1896, when only eight performances had been originally scheduled. Though Puccini was to endure still more indifference from the cognoscenti after the Rome and Naples premieres, he had only to wait until April to taste absolute triumph, when he traveled to Palermo for the first Sicilian production, after which he took repeated bows to thunderous ovations. So enthusiastic was *that* opening-night audience that the singers had to be called back to the stage in their street clothes to repeat the finale, even though half of the orchestra members had gone home. Within a year, *La Bohème* would be enthusiastically applauded in Buenos Aires, Alexandria, Moscow, Lisbon, Manchester, Berlin, Rio de Janeiro, Mexico City, London, Vienna, Los Angeles, and the Hague. In a sense, the applause has never stopped.

Why is *La Bohème* considered the quintessential opera? There are obvious reasons. For one thing, the opera tells an indelibly touching story with universal appeal, a story heightened and ennobled by the deft melodic expression of Puccini's score. For another, it is a tightly focused musical drama, divided into four acts that are short, accessible, and highly watchable, none of them lasting a second longer than necessary. The opera's allure lies as well in its setting—a rollicking "scene" of dashing young artists, dreamers, and "wannabes" in the Paris of Victor Hugo and Honoré de Balzac, living, loving, and dying in the raw splendor of the moment—a milieu which Puccini knew something of from his own student days in Milan. The

LA VIE DE BOHÊME

DRAME EN CINQ ACTES

PAR

THÉODORE BARRIÈRE ET HENRY MURGER

REPRÉSENTÉ POUR LA PREMIÈRE FOIS, A PARIS, SUR LE THÉATRE DES VARIÉTÉS, LE 22 NOVEMBRE 1849
ET REPRIS SUR LE THÉATRE DE L'ODÉON, LE 9 MAI 1873

DISTRIBUTION DE LA PIÈCE

	VARIÉTÉS.	ODÉON.		VARIÉTÉS.	ODÉON.
DURANDIN, homme d'affaires.....	MM. DESSERT.	MM. NOEL MARTIN.	UN MONSIEUR	MM. CHARLES.	MM. FRÉVILLE.
RODOLPHE, son neveu, poète.....	P. LABA.	P. BERTON.	UN MÉDECIN...........		ROUAL.	VALBEL.
MARCEL, peintre............	DARTIGNY.	POREL.	CÉSARINE DE ROUVRE, jeune veuve..	Mme MARGUET.	Mme DEFRANAKL.
SCHAUNARD, musicien.........	CH. PÉREY.	G. RICHARD.	MIMI................	TOUILLIER.	E. BROISAT.
GUSTAVE COLLINE, philosophe	METEL.	CLEAR.	MUSETTE.............	PAGE.	L. LEBLANC.
M. BENOIT, maître d'hôtel.......	BARDOU jeune	RICHARD.	PHÉMIE..............	P. POTEL.	FAISY.
BAPTISTE, domestique.........	KOPP.	FRANÇOIS.	UNE DAME............	WILHEM.	NOÉMIE.
UN GARÇON DE CAISSE........	GALLIN.	ERNEST.	UN COMMISSIONNAIRE. — DOMESTIQUES DE CÉSARINE. — INVITÉS.		

— Droits de reproduction, de traduction et de représentation réservés —

Playbill for Théodore Barrière's 1873 adaptation of Henri Murger's novel, *Scènes de la vie de Bohème*, on which Giuseppe Giacosa and Luigi Illica based their libretto.

romantic plot is virtually unequaled in its ability to generate immediate empathy in an audience, *any* audience, anywhere in the world.

More intriguing, though, are the reasons for the curious hesitation on the part of the first audiences and critics, the very reasons the opera has enjoyed enduring success.

In Turin, in the last weeks of 1895, audiences heard for the first time Richard Wagner's *Götterdämmerung*, with Toscanini conducting—an experience that left them thrilled but overwhelmed, struggling to grasp its lofty ideals and follow the new direction in which it seemed to be leading opera. And then, out of the blue, came *La Bohème*—a finely crafted opera, to be sure, but one devoid of spectacle or intellectual pretension. Short, fleetfooted, and to-the-point, full of raucous humor and emotional hairpin turns, almost shocking in its sexual candor, and populated with life-size characters who might have wandered in off the streets—could this opera be a part of the same elevated medium as Wagner's or, indeed, Verdi's?

The answer is yes. Building on what he had learned from both composers, Puccini was determined to create a fluid and energetic musical drama that would realize Henri Murger's modest episodic novel, *Scènes de la vie de bohème*, in subtle and sensitive detail. Those first, privileged audiences who heard *La Bohème* probably were nonplused that the opera, compelling and sophisticated as it seemed to be, was about something so . . . well, *ordinary*. Puccini may have been alone

The award-winning musical *Rent* was inspired by *La Bohème*.

in appreciating the fact that ordinary did not have to mean banal, that it could, in fact, be disarming in its eloquence. Other operas in the then-popular style of realism called verismo dealt with ordinary people. Ruggero Leoncavallo's *I pagliacci* and Mascagni's *Cavalleria rusticana* shocked and delighted audiences in the early 1890s with their tales of lust and revenge among the poor and downtrodden, but they were essentially as melodramatic, bloody, and frenzied as the most typical Italian opera of the nineteenth century. *La Bohème* would be very different: an opera that took its character and scale from the small, inconsequential details that make everyday life, in retrospect, a provocative, touching, and occasionally heartrending common experience.

La Bohème casts a spell that has yet to be broken. Almost a century to the day, after the opera's world premiere, the New York theater world was entranced by the first performance of an inventive new musical called *Rent*, inspired by and based on *La Bohème*. Now set on New York's Lower East Side, Murger's characters and Puccini's score have been transformed in a modern age of relative freedom that is clouded with the threat of AIDS. *Rent* was the work of composer-lyricist-librettist Jonathan Larson, a perfectionist in search of a new expressive style who died suddenly just before his show opened off-off-Broadway. As if to echo the backstage story of *La Bohème*, the success of *Rent* took the New York cognoscenti completely by surprise. Within three months it had moved to Broadway with huge fanfare and record advance ticket sales and won Larson a posthumous Pulitzer Prize in drama.

An early advertising poster for *La Bohème*.

Puccini's success in *La Bohème* was so unique—and it was *his* success, for he drove his librettists Giuseppe Giacosa and Luigi Illica to the point of mutiny to get precisely what he wanted—that it might even be seen as a prototype for another phenomenon that was only a few years in the future. In *La Bohème*, Puccini had created the first great feature-length film.

Of course, there were no feature-length sound movies when Puccini, Giacosa, and Illica were writing *La Bohème*. That kind of technical sophistication was some forty years in the future. (There was, however, a beautiful silent film of *La Bohème* made in 1926, with Lillian Gish as the heroine Mimì.) But their realization of the story is best described as cinematic in its impact. They synthesized plot, dialogue, music, pace, atmosphere, and visual detail into an unusually lean, well-integrated, and propulsive narrative. Puccini the composer acts as the director, so to speak, with his score serving to adjust the perspective, intensify the mood, isolate the details, and link them to the action. He moves the "camera," choosing the close-ups and staging the master shots, controlling the dynamic range and flow of energy in the story. Though it seems quaint and even friendly

Inside Cafè Momus in a 1930 Metropolitan Opera production.

now, *La Bohème* unnerved its first audiences because it dared
to be genuine, unvarnished, unpretentious—in short, real in
a way that few operatic love stories had ever been.

Puccini's is not the only opera called *La Bohème*. Sometime
in early 1893, Ruggero Leoncavallo (1857–1919) had appar-
ently decided to base an opera on the French writer Murger's
celebrated novel and the popular play that Théodore Barrière
had adapted from it. Though Puccini had recently enjoyed
his first solid success with the debut of his third opera *Manon
Lescaut*, Leoncavallo was a much bigger name in Italian opera
at that time. His *I pagliacci* had taken the world by storm the
year before, and Leoncavallo was seriously considered, if only

briefly, the most likely candidate to assume the mantle of Italian opera's undisputed master, the aging Giuseppe Verdi. Puccini and Leoncavallo were friends from their conservatory days in Milan, and Leoncavallo was one of a succession of people who had tried to bring some order to the troublesome libretto for Puccini's *Manon Lescaut.*

In a casual encounter in Milan in March of 1893, Puccini told Leoncavallo that he intended to write an opera based on the Murger novel and the Barrière play. Leoncavallo was first shocked and then furious. Not only was he already at work on such an opera but he insisted that it was *he* who had first mentioned the property to Puccini. Other sources indicate that Giacosa and Illica—both who had finally whipped the *Manon Lescaut* libretto into shape and would become Puccini's finest librettists—had decided to write a libretto for *La Bohème* even before the *Manon Lescaut* premiere. But history is unclear on who actually had the idea first. Since Leoncavallo did not premiere his version of *La Bohème* until 1897, he could not have had much of a headstart when he learned of Puccini's

Ruggero Leoncavallo (1858–1919) was enraged when Pucini decided to develop *La Bohème*, an opera he had already begun working on.

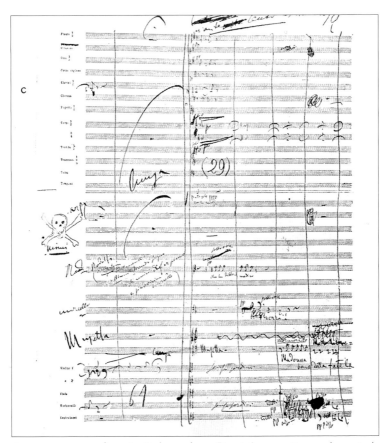

A manuscript page from *La Bohème* shows Puccini's corrections and marginal drawings.

plans in the winter of 1893. Still, his publisher Sonzogno mounted a publicity campaign to convince the public that the idea for such an opera belonged exclusively to Leoncavallo.

In an interview in the Milan newspaper *Corriere della Sera*, Puccini stated that he did not know of his friend Leoncavallo's intentions until their fateful meeting, and that now, of course, it was "too late" for him to drop his plans. He added, in a challenge that must have enraged Leoncavallo, that the public should ultimately decide who had written the better opera.

The public did decide. Puccini and his librettists worked relentlessly for three years on *La Bohème* and beat Leoncavallo to the stage by well over a year. Despite the hesitant reaction of its first audience, the opera quickly became a runaway hit. Leoncavallo proved to be something of a one–trick pony, never able to equal the enduring success of *I pagliacci*, despite the popularity of several of his operas in his lifetime. His version of *La Bohème*—quite different in plot and structure from Puccini's—contained some lovely passages and, though not a failure, the polite praise it received seemed to damn it, as the entire world appeared to go mad for Puccini's opera. Leoncavallo's anger over what he considered betrayal by Puccini turned into profound bitterness, and ended their friendship. As his star began to fall, Puccini's rose.

Did Puccini steal the idea from Leoncavallo? It is possible. He had the nerve, after all, to make an opera of Abbé Prevost's novel *Manon Lescaut* less than a decade after the debut of French composer Jules Massenet's hugely successful *Manon*. And, in choosing to follow *La Bohème* with *Tosca*, Puccini had to wrest the exclusive rights to Victorien Sardou's play *La Tosca* away from another celebrated Italian composer of the day, Alberto Franchetti. Puccini's behavior in these matters could be callous, cruel, and breathtakingly arrogant, but he had the one quality that, in an artist, can forgive the rest—genius.

Giacomo Puccini was born in the Italian town of Lucca on December 22, 1858. He represented the fifth generation of a dynasty of musicians who had dominated the city's musical life for over a century. Puccini was only five when his father Michele died, and it was his mother Albina who saw to it that the eldest son carried on the family tradition. The boy was hardly enthusiastic. Far more interested in fun and games, he was a poor student who showed no inclination at all for the rigors of musical study. Only when he was sent to Lucca's Instituto Musicale Pacini, to be taught by a former student of his father's, did Puccini discover that he was interested in music. That interest quickly turned into a passion. The teenager became a passably good pianist and organist who still had a fondness for trickery; as an inside joke, while serving as a church organist in Lucca, he was known to weave popular secular songs into the music he played for the services. He began composing when he was seventeen but the turning point in his development came the following year, when he saw a performance of *Aida* in Pisa. It convinced him that his future lay in writing for the theater.

In 1880, after graduating from the Lucca conservatory, Puccini received a stipend that allowed him to move to Milan to study composition at that city's conservatory with Antonio Bazzini and Amilcare Ponchielli, the young, respected composer of *La Gioconda*. Puccini's three years as a student in Milan shaped him as a composer, and his threadbare existence as a

poor student appears to have made him particularly sympathetic to the characters and situations he would encounter in Murger's *Scènes de la vie de bohème.* His graduation exercise, an orchestral work called *Capriccio sinfonico,* won him warm praise and it, too, would play an important role in *La Bohème*—the vigorous orchestral openings to the opera's first and last acts were lifted from that student work.

It was Ponchielli who brought Puccini together with his first librettist, Ferdinando Fontana. Together they wrote *Le villi* (1884), a short opera that failed to win a prize but that did attract favorable notice and the attention of Giulio Ricordi, the head of the formidable Ricordi publishing empire, which published all of Verdi's operas and was a dominant force in Italian opera throughout the nineteenth and twentieth centuries. Ricordi commissioned an opera from Puccini, and, after five years, Puccini and Fontana came up with *Edgar,* a turgid three-act drama that contains a great deal of beautiful music. Reaction to the 1889 premiere at La Scala, Milan, was lukewarm, convincing the supremely confident Puccini that even he could not prevail against a weak or inept libretto.

When he set to work on *Manon Lescaut,* he was determined to fight for the libretto he needed. Writers came and went until he found a productive relationship through Giulio Ricordi with Giuseppe Giacosa (1847–1906) and Luigi Illica (1857–1919). They methodically went about their work in a way that impressed Puccini. Generally, Illica dealt with the mechanics of plot and narrative, while Giacosa concentrated on writing the actual text, though their tasks in the partnership frequently varied. Their efficient and compelling work spoke for itself. *Manon Lescaut* was a triumph, and the composer and librettists decided to continue their collaboration with *La Bohème.*

Puccini was a master of musical drama, as seen in the setting of *La Bohème* at the Lyric Opera of Chicago.

The creation of *La Bohème* was an arduous and combative process. Puccini drove Giacosa and Illica to distraction with his fanatical insistence on a tightly woven plot and precise articulation of the text. They fought bitterly, but when the librettists heard the score Puccini had written—with its subtle, reflexive, and infinitely sensitive handling of mood and emotion—they understood why he pushed so relentlessly. He was right when he exhorted them, "Simplify, simplify." Puccini understood that text and plot could only go so far in opera, that music would seal the drama, and that the ideal libretto provided the composer with the necessary foundation for what, in the end, was a *musical* drama.

The overwhelming international success of *Manon Lescaut* and *La Bohème* made Puccini a very wealthy man, a celebrity, and the leader of a generation of composers that, in addition to the wounded Leoncavallo, included Pietro Mascagni (*Cavalleria rusticana*), Umberto Giordano (*Andrea Chénier*), and Francesco Cilea (*Adriana Lecouvreur*). His next opera, *Tosca* (1900), was another success, as was *Madama Butterfly* (1904), both written in collaboration with Giacosa and Illica. Incidentally, the La Scala premiere of *Madama Butterfly* was an out-and-out disaster. The audience, provoked by a group jealous of Puccini's success, jeered the opera and subjected the composer to his first humiliation in the theater. Furious, Puccini withdrew the score and attacked the problems the opera seemed to have in its premiere; the revised version that reached the stage three months later was a revelation, and *Madama Butterfly* joined his earlier successes as an international hit.

In the remaining twenty years of his life, Puccini never quite matched the astonishing run he achieved with those four successive hits, though several of his later operas—especially *La fanciulla del West*, the original "spaghetti Western," written for the Metropolitan Opera in 1910; the wicked and dazzling one-act comedy *Gianni Schicchi*; and the epic *Turandot*, left unfinished at his death—are eminently worthy of comparison. The depth of Puccini's talent is reflected in the painstaking study and

An EMI recording session of *La Bohème*. Seated in foreground are Nicolai Gedda on left and Thomas Schippers in center; in background, Mario Sereni leaning over table and Mirella Freni seated at far right.

effort he lavished on the task of composing *Turandot*, even though he began to work on it when he was in his sixties and suffering from the cancer that would kill him in 1924. Yet for all the sophistication and invention as a composer that he displayed in his later years, Puccini never again portrayed human passion as perceptively as he did in *La Bohème*. The brilliant stage managing of *Tosca* and the deft manipulation of *Madama Butterfly* remind us, from time to time, that we are in the hands of a shrewd master craftsman, instinctive entertainer, and consummate musical dramatist. In *La Bohème*, the artifice is invisible. Each turn of phrase seems as inevitable as breathing. The result, for once, is not opera. It is poetry.

THE STORY OF THE OPERA

Act 1

On Christmas Eve, in the year 1830, two passionate young bohemian artists—a poet named Rodolfo and a painter named Marcello—busy themselves with work in their studio apartment in the garret of a house in the Latin quarter of Paris. Neither is really getting much done, but the effort at least takes their minds off the bitter cold and the fact that they don't have any fuel for their stove. Rodolfo finally decides to burn his manuscript to provide some heat. Their friend, a philosopher named Colline, arrives just in time to savor the warmth, but the fire does not last long, and when it dies out, Colline and Marcello boo its author.

At that moment, two boys burst in bearing abundant gifts that seem too good to be true—food, wine, and fuel for the stove. The source of this bounty is the musician Schaunard, the fourth member of this quartet of hapless idealists, who

Marcello and Rodolfo in their tiny garret.

bursts in with a wild tale about how he wound up with a pock-
etful of money, which he tosses on the table. While his friends
are happy for him, they are more interested in eating, drink-
ing, and building a hearty fire than in hearing his story. Realizing
that his good will has upstaged his own story, Schaunard suggests that they go out to eat, since it is Christmas Eve and he
is—for the moment, anyway—flush with money.

Their departure is delayed by the unexpected arrival of the
old landlord Benoit. The rent, which they don't have, is due.
Marcello invites Benoit into the apartment, letting him see
the money Schaunard has left on the table, and offers him a
drink. All four of the bohemians play up to Benoit, making
him feel like "one of the boys" and manage to convince him

to tell outrageous stories of his way with women. The landlord lets it slip that he is married, at which point the bohemians turn on him in a show of fake indignation that he takes so seriously that he flees the garret without giving another thought to the rent.

Rodolfo sends the others ahead to wait for him downstairs so he can finish an article he is writing. Once he is alone, though, he realizes that he is in no mood to write. A knock at the door stirs him. It is his neighbor, the frail and consumptive Mimì, who asks him to light her candle. When she enters the garret, Mimì almost collapses, dropping both the candle and the key to her room. Alarmed, Rodolfo relights her candle. Mimì is about to leave when she realizes that her key is missing. A sudden draft of cold air once again extinguishes her candle and, seeing his opportunity, Rodolfo quietly blows his out as well. In the darkness, they search for the key, which Rodolfo soon finds and pockets. A moment later, he touches Mimì's chilled hand,

Renata Tebaldi, the Italian soprano discovered by Toscanini, as Mimì.

which he offers to warm. He introduces himself and admits that she has stolen his heart. She, in turn, reveals herself to Rodolfo: her real name is Lucia, she makes artificial flowers, and she hungers for the arrival of spring. Time seems to stand still. When the bohemians shout up to the garret from the street, Rodolfo tells them to go ahead to the Café Momus, where he will join them. As he turns back from the window, he sees Mimì standing in a shaft of moonlight, appearing indescribably beautiful to him. Both are overcome by the realization that they are in love, and she suggests they leave to join the bohemians. Rodolfo asks Mimì about what might happen later, after dinner, and she teasingly tells him to wait and see. They leave, arm in arm, enraptured . . . and, at last, oblivious to the cold.

Act 2

The street outside the Café Momus is thronged with shoppers, diners, and street vendors. On their way to dinner, Rodolfo has bought a pink bonnet for Mimì in a millinery shop. When the couple arrives at the café, the bohemians greet Mimì with deep bows and mock gallantry, making her laugh and feel

Dance at Bougival by Pierre Auguste Renoir.

immediately welcome. All this good will curdles with the arrival of Musetta, a dazzling girl who has recently broken Marcello's heart by dumping him for a rich, older man, Alcindoro. Musetta sweeps in, trailed by the frantic Alcindoro, and takes a table near the bohemians. This is no coincidence: Musetta, realizing that Marcello is nearby, begins to taunt him mercilessly by making a show of herself, which mortifies Alcindoro and makes Marcello seethe. The other bohemians fill Mimì in on the details of that romance, which amuse her and remind her suddenly of how deeply she loves Rodolfo. Desperate to get rid of Alcindoro, Musetta screams as if her foot were in pain. The old man leaps about to mollify her, finally running off to the cobbler with her offending shoe as she falls into the arms of the utterly beguiled Marcello. When the bill comes, the bohemians realize they have spent all of Schaunard's money and cannot pay for dinner. Suddenly, a military parade marches in. In the frenzy, the bohemians tag along and march off, leaving the bill, which is presented to Alcindoro when he returns to the empty café.

Act 3

A couple of months pass, and Paris is buried in the depths of winter. On a freezing February morning, Mimì turns up at an inn near the Barrière d'Enfer, one of the gates of the city of Paris. Marcello and Musetta are living at a nearby inn, and Mimì—whose poor health is becoming ever more apparent—has come to ask Marcello for advice about Rodolfo. Their passionate love affair has become turbulent, and Rodolfo's jealousy is threatening their future. Marcello tells Mimì she should leave him and reveals that Rodolfo is actually asleep inside the inn, having turned up earlier that morning. When Rodolfo emerges, Mimì hides. He explains to Marcello that he has been jealous because Mimì is a coquette, but finally admits that Mimì is seriously, perhaps fatally ill, and his heart is breaking at the thought of losing her. In the shadows, Mimì is seized with a fit of coughing and the devastated Rodolfo rushes to her side. From inside the inn's tavern, a scream from Musetta distracts Marcello, who rushes in to deal with her. When they are alone, Mimì quietly tells Rodolfo that she is

The street outside Cafè Momus in a Metropolitan Opera production.

leaving him. She tells him to gather her possessions, but they later agree to stay together until the spring, reaching an understanding just as Marcello and Musetta burst out of the tavern, their vigorous fighting providing an ironic counterpoint to the sorrow of Mimì and Rodolfo.

Musetta's ploy as depicted in a 1993 production at the Santa Fe opera.

Act 4

With the arrival of spring, Marcello and Rodolfo are back in their Parisian garret, once more struggling to look busy. Newly single, they are trying to avoid thinking about the women they have loved and lost. Idle talk about their work turns to gossip about Mimì and Musetta and wondering what has become of them. Colline and Schaunard turn up with the makings of a modest supper. The distraction is so welcome that the joking turns into a wild improvised melodrama, complete with cross dressing and a duel fought with loaves of bread.

In the midst of the commotion, the door flies open to reveal Musetta, who is frantic. She has left Mimì waiting downstairs and tells

Enrico Caruso as Rodolfo.

them that Mimì is now so frail that she cannot even climb the steps, that she knew of nowhere else to go. Rodolfo rushes out to find Mimì and carry her upstairs while the others create a place for her to rest. They have nothing to offer her, so Musetta sends Marcello off with her earrings to pay for food, a doctor, and some medicine. She decides to join him, so she can buy a muff to warm Mimì's hands. Colline decides to pawn his beloved overcoat, and he urges Schaunard to come along so Rodolfo and Mimì can have some time alone. The lovers savor their moment together, recalling their first meeting and how suddenly and completely they fell in love. One by one, the others return from their missions. Rodolfo busies himself arranging the drapes, and the exhausted Mimì falls asleep. Musetta alone knows how sick Mimì is, and she kneels in fervent prayer. But it is too late. When Colline returns and asks about Mimì, none of the others can even form the words to answer him. When Rodolfo attempts to offer an optimistic answer, he realizes what the awful silence and his friends' stricken faces mean. Mimì is dead. Marcello embraces Rodolfo and tells him to be courageous, but the poet is shattered, collapsing over Mimì's lifeless body and crying out her name as the others watch in sorrow.

Mimì (Angela Gheorghiu) and Rodolfo (Roberto Alagna) savor their last moments together in 1996 production at the Metropolitan Opera.

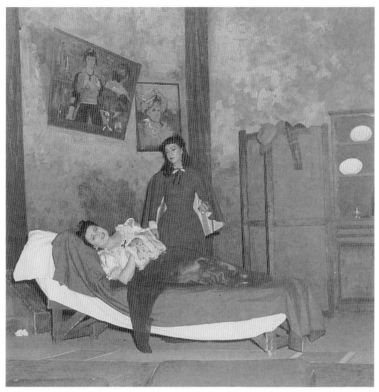

Musetta (Patrice Munsel) comforts an ailing Mimì (Victoria de Los Angeles) in the 1951 Metropolitan Opera production of *La Bohème*.

THE PERFORMERS

Nicolai Gedda (Rodolfo) has become the model of the modern tenor, equally at home on opera, recital, and concert stages, a sophisticated singer equipped with a firm but flexible technique that has allowed him to perform a repertoire almost unprecedented in its breadth. He was born in Stockholm in 1925 to a Swedish mother and a Russian father (who was a bass in the Don Cossack Choir) and spent part of his childhood in Leipzig. His gift for languages was a key factor in his early success. Gedda made his professional debut in Stockholm in 1952 in the title role of Adolphe Adam's *Le Postillon de Longjumeau*. Walter Legge of EMI Records happened to hear Gedda during a Stockholm visit that year and, noting his linguistic skill as well as his brilliant lyric tenor voice, immediately signed him for an upcoming recording of *Boris Godunov*. Major European debuts followed quickly, as Gedda established himself with a succession of important recordings for EMI. In addition to opera, he was recognized as a distinguished *lieder* singer and oratorio soloist. In the year following

Nicolai Gedda as Rodolfo.

his 1957 Metropolitan Opera debut, he created the title role in the company's world premiere of Samuel Barber's *Vanessa*. For the next thirty years, Gedda sang operatic roles as diverse as the boyish Nemorino in *L'Elisir d'amore* and the heroic title part in Wagner's *Lohengrin*. Later in his career, he took on Russian roles and explored unusual areas of the song repertoire, with occasional forays into novelty, singing, for instance, on composer-conductor Leonard Bernstein's definitive recording of the musical *Candide*.

MIRELLA FRENI (Mimì) was born in 1935 in Modena, a few months earlier than the city's most famous son, Luciano Pavarotti. As infants, the two singers-to-be—who would later become affectionate colleagues—shared the same wet nurse, and their mothers worked in the same cigarette factory. Freni began studying voice with her uncle, making her first public

Mirella Freni as Mimì in her 1965 Metropolitan Opera debut.

appearance at the age of eleven with another prodigy, the pianist Leone Magiera, who would become her first husband. She made her opera debut in 1955 in Modena as Micaëla in *Carmen*, inaugurating what would be a stellar international stage and recording career of extraordinary range and longevity. After singing several seasons with provincial Italian houses, Freni made strong impressions in debuts with the Amsterdam Opera (1959), London's Covent Garden (1961), and Milan's La Scala (1962), quickly becoming one of Europe's most sought-after lyric sopranos. The role of Mimì became her calling card, especially after her performance in the successful 1963 film of Franco Zeffirelli's La Scala production, conducted by Herbert von Karajan. Freni sang Mimì in her debuts at Moscow's Bolshoi Opera (1964) and New York's Metropolitan Opera (1965). She also excelled in such roles as Susanna in *Le nozze di Figaro*, Violetta in *La traviata*, Zerlina in *Don Giovanni*, Marguerite in *Faust*, and Juliette in *Roméo et Juliette*. In the 1970s, when Freni decided to sing heavier roles—a dangerous choice for a lyric soprano—many critics predicted that it would ruin her voice. Bolstered by a steady technique and the sensitive support of conductors such as von Karajan and Riccardo Muti, she was instead acclaimed for bringing a distinctive lyrical warmth to performances and recordings of the title role in *Aida*, Cio-Cio-San in *Madama Butterfly*, Elisabetta in *Don Carlo*, and Leonora in *La forza del destino*. In 1981, she married the Bulgarian bass Nicolai Ghiaurov, a colleague who virtually became her professional partner, notably after

Freni began singing Russian roles such as Tatyana in *Eugene Onegin*. In the 1990s, she has been noted for her performances in the demanding prima donna roles of such verismo warhorses as *Adriana Lecouvreur* and *Fedora*.

Mario Sereni as Marcello.

MARIO SERENI (Marcello) enjoyed great popularity in the 1950s and 1960s in the important baritone roles of the Italian repertoire, both in major international houses and on recordings. Born in Perugia, Italy, in 1928, Sereni attended Rome's Accademia de Santa Cecilia and the Accademia Chigiana in Siena, where he was the student of Mario Basiola. His professional career began in 1953 on an unusually high level—at the Maggio Musicale Fiorentino (Florence May Festival)—and within four years, he had made his Metropolitan Opera debut as Gérard in *Andrea Chénier* and had also sung at Buenos Aires's Teatro Colón. Sereni enjoyed a long and steady career at the Metropolitan Opera, London's Covent Garden, Milan's La Scala, the Vienna Staatsoper, and other companies around the world. Despite his success, Sereni remained in the shadow of the more charismatic baritones of his time—principally Leonard Warren, Tito Gobbi, Robert Merrill, Ettore Bastianini, Piero Cappuccilli, and Rolando Panerai—and critics of the time frequently dismissed his singing. Yet his many recordings (he can be heard on the legendary *Lisbon Traviata* recording of 1958 with Maria Callas and Alfredo Kraus) reveal a singer and musician of considerable distinction, with a handsome voice, a durable technique, and a fine sense of style.

THOMAS SCHIPPERS (1930–1977) was a prodigiously gifted American conductor whose professional career began only a few days after his twentieth birthday, when he led the New York premiere of Gian Carlo Menotti's *The Consul*. Born in Kalamazoo, Michigan, Schippers made his public debut as a pianist

at the age of six and became a church organist when he was fourteen. He attended the Curtis Institute of Music and Yale University, where he took composition lessons from Paul Hindemith. At the age of eighteen, he won second prize in a conducting competition sponsored by the Philadelphia Orchestra. Schippers's career really took off, though, through his work with Menotti; in addition to *The Consul* premiere, he conducted the 1951 television premiere of Menotti's *Amahl and the Night Visitors* and, a year later, made his New York City Opera debut at the helm of Menotti's *The Old Maid and the Thief.* He remained at New York City Opera until 1954, then made his New York Philharmonic debut in 1955. That same year he made his Metropolitan Opera debut, the beginning of an association that would last the rest of his life. (It was Schippers who was conducting the 1960 performance of Verdi's *La forza del destino* during which baritone Leonard Warren died onstage.) Rich, young, matinee-idol handsome, well-spoken, and a superb musician, Schippers became the quintessential celebrity conductor in a media-driven age. He joined Leonard Bernstein for the New York Philharmonic's historic visit to the

Gedda and Freni at an EMI recording session of La Bohème.

U.S.S.R. in 1959, conducted the world premiere of Manuel de Falla's *Atlántida* at La Scala in 1962 and, two years later, became one of the youngest conductors in the history of the Bayreuth Festival. In the fall of 1966, Schippers led the world premiere of Samuel Barber's *Antony and Cleopatra*, which officially opened the Metropolitan Opera's new home at Lincoln Center, where he later led the company's first performances of Modest Mussorgsky's original version of *Boris Godunov* and Gioacchino Rossini's *The Siege of Corinth*, which provided Beverly Sills with her Met debut. From 1958 until 1976, the year before his death, he maintained close ties to Menotti's Festival of Two Worlds in Spoleto, Italy. In 1970, Schippers was named conductor of the Cincinnati Symphony Orchestra and later joined the faculty of the city's college conservatory of music. For all his success, Schippers's life ended in suffering: his wife died of cancer in 1973 and he died of the same disease four years later. Unable to continue as conductor of the Cincinnati Symphony Orchestra, Schippers was named its conductor laureate and, in turn, he bequeathed the orchestra five million dollars.

The Libretto

Act 1

A GARRET A large window through which an expanse of snow-covered roofs is seen. At right, a stove. A table, a bed, four chairs, a painter's easel with half-finished canvas books everywhere, manuscripts. Rodolfo is thoughtful, looking out the window. Marcello works at his painting "The Crossing of the Red Sea," his hands stiff with cold; he tries to warm them by blowing on them now and again.

DISC NO. 1/TRACK 1

Questo Mar Rosse **The opera begins with a vigorous melodic subject that Puccini created for his Capriccio sinfonico, written when he was a conservatory student. A whiplash from the orchestra, it plunges the listener immediately into the action. The first act is then off to a gallop, a concentrated whirlwind of activity lasting around twenty minutes that does not stop until the bohemians decide to adjourn the Café Momus. The score responds so articulately to the action (and is just as sensitively orchestrated) that matters of tempo and pace vary from bar to bar, and it must be experienced moment by moment.**

MARCELLO

Questo "Mar Rosso" mi ammollisce
e assidera come se addosso
mi piovesse in stille.
Per vendicarmi affogo un Faraone.

to Rodolfo

Che fai?

RODOLFO

Nei cieli bigi
guardo fumar dai mille
comignoli Parigi,

MARCELLO

This "Red Sea" of mine
makes me feel cold and numb
as if it were pouring over me.
I'll drown a Pharaoh in revenge.

What are you doing?

RODOLFO

I'm looking at Paris,
seeing the skies grey with smoke
from a thousand chimneys,

e penso a quel poltrone
d'un vecchio caminetto ingannatore
che vive in ozio come un gran signor.

MARCELLO
Le sue rendite oneste
da un pezzo non riceve.

RODOLFO
Quelle sciocche foreste
che fan sotto la neve?

MARCELLO
Rodolfo, io voglio dirti
un mio pensier profondo
ho un freddo cane.

RODOLFO
Ed io, Marcel, non ti nascondo
che non credo al sudor della fronte.

and I think of that no-good,
hateful stove of ours that lives
a gentleman's life of idleness.

MARCELLO
It's been a long time
since he received his just income.

RODOLFO
What are those stupid forests
doing, all covered with snow?

MARCELLO
Rodolfo, I want to tell you
a profound thought I've had
I'm cold as hell.

RODOLFO
As for me, Marcello, I'll be frank
I'm not exactly sweating.

Act II of *La Bohème* in a 1993 production at the Santa Fe Opera.

MARCELLO

Ho ghiacciate le dita
quasi ancora le tenessi immollate
giù in quella gran ghiacciaia
che è il cuore di Musetta.

A sigh escapes him, and he leaves off painting.

RODOLFO

L'amore è un caminetto che sciupa
troppo…

MARCELLO

E in fretta!

RODOLFO

Dove l'uomo è fascina.

MARCELLO

E la donna è l'alare…

RODOLFO

L'uno brucia in un soffio…

MARCELLO

E l'altro a guardare…

RODOLFO

Ma intanto que si gela…

MARCELLO

E si muore d'inedia…

RODOLFO

Fuoco ci vuole…

MARCELLO

And my fingers are frozen—
as if I still were holding them
in that enormous glacier,
Musetta's heart.

RODOLFO

Love is a stove that burns too much…

MARCELLO

Too fast!

RODOLFO

Where the man is the fuel…

MARCELLO

And woman the spark…

RODOLFO

He burns in a moment…

MARCELLO

And she stands by, watching!

RODOLFO

Meanwhile, we're freezing in here!

MARCELLO

And dying from lack of food!

RODOLFO

We must have a fire…

MARCELLO (*afferrando una sedia*)
Aspetta…sacrifichiam la sedia

MARCELLO (*seizing a chair*)
Wait…we'll sacrifice the chair!

Rodolfo keeps Marcello from breaking the chair. Suddenly he shouts with joy.

RODOLFO
Eureka!

RODOLFO
Eureka!

MARCELLO
Trovasti?

MARCELLO
You've found it?

RODOLFO
Sì. Aguzza l'ingegno.
L'idea vampi in fiamma.

RODOLFO
Yes. Sharpen your wits.
Let Thought burst into flame.

MARCELLO (*additando il suo quadro*)
Bruciamo il "Mar Rosso"?

MARCELLO (*pointing to his picture*)
Shall we burn the "Red Sea"?

RODOLFO
No. Puzza la tela dipinta.
Il mio dramma…
L'ardente mio dramma ci scaldi.

RODOLFO
No. Painted canvas smells.
My play…
My burning drama will warm us.

MARCELLO
Vuoi leggerlo forse? Mi geli.

MARCELLO
You mean to read it? I'll freeze.

RODOLFO
No, in cener la carta si sfaldi
e l'estro rivoli ai suoi cieli.
Al secol gran danno minaccia…
Ma Roma è in periglio…

RODOLFO
No, the paper will unfold in ash
and genius soar back to its heaven.
A serious loss to the age…
but Rome is in danger…

MARCELLO
Gran cor!

MARCELLO
What a noble heart!

RODOLFO	**RODOLFO**
A te l'atto primo!	Here, take the first act!
MARCELLO	**MARCELLO**
Qua.	Here.
RODOLFO	**RODOLFO**
Straccia.	Tear it up.
MARCELLO	**MARCELLO**
Accendi.	Light it.

Rodolfo lights the part of the manuscript thrown in the fire. Then the two friends draw up chairs and sit down, voluptuously warming themselves.

RODOLFO E MARCELLO	**RODOLFO AND MARCELLO**
Che lieto baglior	What blissful heat!

The door opens and Colline enters, frozen, stamping his feet. He throws some books on the table.

COLLINE	**COLLINE**
Già dell'Apocalisse appariscono i segni.	Signs of the Apocalypse begin to appear.
In giorno di Vigilia non si accettano pegni!	No pawning allowed on Christmas Eve.

surprised

Una fiammata!	A fire!
RODOLFO	**RODOLFO**
Zitto, si dà il mio dramma…	Quiet, my play's being given…
MARCELLO	**MARCELLO**
…al fuoco.	…to the stove.

COLLINE

Lo trovo scintillante.

RODOLFO

Vivo.

MARCELLO

Ma dura poco.

RODOLFO

La brevità, gran pregio.

COLLINE

Autore, a me la sedia.

MARCELLO

Questi intermezzi
fan morir d'inedia.
Presto!

RODOLFO

Atto secondo.

MARCELLO

Non far sussurro.

COLLINE

I find it full of fire.

RODOLFO

Brilliant.

MARCELLO

But brief.

RODOLFO

Brevity, its great merit.

COLLINE

Your chair, please, Mr. Author.

MARCELLO

These intermissions
kill you with boredom.
Get on with it!

RODOLFO

Act two.

MARCELLO

No whispering.

DISC NO. 1/TRACK 2

The imposing Colline joins the friends in the garret, and engages in the mock-heroic banter that is the hallmark of this arty crowd. The orchestra imitates the sounds of fire while the friends watch Rodolfo's play burn in the stove, typical of the attention and importance given to life's details throughout this score.

COLLINE

Pensier profondo!

COLLINE

What profundity!

MARCELLO

Giusto color!

MARCELLO

How colorful!

RODOLFO

In quell'azzurro guizzo languente
sfuma un'ardente scena d'amor.

RODOLFO

In that dying blue flame
an ardent love-scene dies.

COLLINE

Scoppietta un foglio.

COLLINE

See that page crackle.

MARCELLO

Là c'eran baci!

MARCELLO

There were the kisses!

RODOLFO

Tre atti or voglio d'un colpo udir.

RODOLFO

I want to hear three acts at once.

He throws the rest of the manuscript on the fire.

COLLINE

Tal degli audaci l'idea s'integra.

COLLINE

And so unified is your bold conception.

TUTTI

Bello in allegra vampa svanir.

ALL

Beautiful death on the joyful flame.

They applaud. Then the flame dies.

MARCELLO

Oh! Dio…già s'abbassa la fiamma.

MARCELLO

Oh Lord! The flame is dying.

COLLINE

Che vano, che fragile dramma!

COLLINE

So useless, so fragile a drama!

MARCELLO

Già scricchiola, increspasi, muor.

MARCELLO

Already curling up to die.

COLLINE E MARCELLO	COLLINE AND MARCELLO
Abbasso, abbasso l'autore.	Down with the author!

Two porters come in, one carrying food, bottles of wine and cigars; the other has a bundle of wood. At the sound, the three men in front of the fire turn around and with shouts of amazement fall upon the provisions.

DISC NO. 1/TRACK 3

The appearance of Schaunard and his bounty lifts the friends's spirits, marked by faster tempi in the score. Schaunard's description of the pleasures of the Latin Quarter (02:51) will become a motif heard at key moments throughout the opera.

RODOLFO	RODOLFO
Legna!	Wood!

MARCELLO	MARCELLO
Sigari!	Cigars!

COLLINE	COLLINE
Bordò!	Bordeaux!

RODOLFO	RODOLFO
Legna!	Firewood!

MARCELLO	MARCELLO
Bordò!	Bordeaux!

TUTTI	ALL THREE
Le dovizie d'una fiera	Destiny provides us
il destin ci destinò…	with a feast of plenty!

The porters leave. Schaunard enters triumphantly, throwing some coins on the floor.

SCHAUNARD	**SCHAUNARD**
La Banca di Francia	The Bank of France
per voi si sbilancia.	has gone broke just for you.
COLLINE *(raccattando gli scudi insieme agli altri)*	**COLLINE** *(gathering up coins, with the others)*
Raccatta, raccatta!	Pick them up!
MARCELLO	**MARCELLO**
Son pezzi di latta!…	They must be made of tin!…
SCHAUNARD	**SCHAUNARD**
Sei sordo?…sei lippo?	Are you deaf? or blind?
showing a crown	
Quest'uomo chi è?	Who is this man?
RODOLFO	**RODOLFO**
Luigi Filippo!	Louis Philippe!
M'inchino al mio Re!	I bow to my King!
TUTTI	**ALL**
Sta Luigi Filippo ai nostri piè!	Louis Philippe is at our feet!

Schaunard wants to tell his adventure, but the others won't listen to him. They set the provisions on the table and put wood in the stove.

SCHAUNARD	**SCHAUNARD**
Or vi dirò questo'oro,	Now I'll tell you this gold,
o meglio, argento	this silver, rather
ha la sua brava istoria…	has a noble history…
RODOLFO	**RODOLFO**
Riscaldiamo il camino!	Let's fire the stove!

COLLINE
Tanto freddo ha sofferto

SCHAUNARD
Un inglese…un signor…lord
o milord che sia, volea un musicista…

MARCELLO
Via! Prepariamo la tavola!

SCHAUNARD
Io? Volo!…

RODOLFO
L'esca dov'è

COLLINE
Là.

MARCELLO
Qua.

SCHAUNARD
…e mi presento.
M'accetta, gli domando…

COLLINE
Arrosto freddo.

MARCELLO
Pasticcio dolce.

SCHAUNARD
…A quando le lezioni?
Mi presento, m'accetta,

COLLINE
It's hard to endure so much cold!

SCHAUNARD
An Englishman…a gentleman…
A lord…was looking for a musician…

MARCELLO
Come! Let's set the table!

SCHAUNARD
And I? I flew to him…

RODOLFO
Where are the matches?

COLLINE
There.

MARCELLO
Here.

SCHAUNARD
…I introduce myself.
He hires me. I ask him…

COLLINE
Cold roast beef.

MARCELLO
Sweet pastry.

SCHAUNARD
When do the lessons begin?…
I introduce myself, he hires me.

gli domando A quando le lezioni?
Risponde "Incominciam…
guardare!" e un pappagallo
m'addita al primo pian.
Poi soggiunge "Voi suonare
finché quello morire!"

RODOLFO
Fulgida folgori la sala splendida!

MARCELLO
Ora le candele.

SCHAUNARD
E fu così
suonai tre lunghi dì…
Allora usai l'incanto
di mia presenza bella…
Affascinai l'ancella…
Gli propinai prezzemolo…

MARCELLO
Mangiar senza tovaglia?

RODOLFO
No un'idea!

He takes a newspaper from his pocket.

MARCELLO E COLLINE
Il Costituzional!

RODOLFO
Ottima carta…
Si mangia e si divora un'appendice!

I ask When do the lessons begin?
He replies "Let's start…
look!" and points to a parrot
on the first floor.
Then adds; "You play
until that bird dies!"

RODOLFO
The dining room's brilliant!

MARCELLO
Now the candles.

SCHAUNARD
And so it went
I played for three long days…
Then I used my charm,
my handsome figure…
I won the serving-girl over…
We poisoned a little parsley…

MARCELLO
Eat without a tablecloth?

RODOLFO
No! I've an idea.

MARCELLO AND COLLINE
The Constitutional!

RODOLFO
Excellent paper…
You eat and devour the news!

SCHAUNARD

Lorito allargò l'ali,
Lorito il becco aprì,
un poco di prezzemolo;
da Socrate morì!

COLLINE *(a Schaunard)*
Chi? …

SCHAUNARD

Il diavolo vi porti tutti quanti…
Ed or che fate?
No! queste cibarie
sono la salmeria
pei dì futuri
tenebrosi e oscuri.
Pranzare in casa il dì della Vigilia
mentre il Quartier Latino le sue vie
addobba di salsicce e leccornie?
Quando un olezzo di frittelle imbalsama le
vecchie strade?
Là le ragazze cantano contente…

TUTTI
La vigilia di Natal!

SCHAUNARD

Ed han per eco, ognuna uno studente!
Un po' di religione, o miei signori
si beva in casa, ma si pranzi fuor…

They pour the wine. A knock at the door.

SCHAUNARD

Lorito spread his wings,
Lorito opened his beak,
took a peck of parsley,
and died like Socrates!

COLLINE *(to Schaunard)*
Who?

SCHAUNARD

Go to the devil, all of you…
Now what are you doing?
No! These delicacies
are the provender
for the dark and gloomy
days in the future.
Dine at home on Christmas Eve
when the Latin Quarter
has decked its streets with eatables?
When the perfume of fritters
is wafted through the ancient streets?
There the girls sing happily…

ALL
It's Christmas Eve!

SCHAUNARD

And each has a student echoing her!
Have some religion, gentlemen
we drink at home, but we dine out.

This comical interlude with the fussy old landlord and his blunt request, "Rent!" shows us the bohemians in action: rhetorical fourishes mix with the risqué (02:14), while they remain sharp-witted and able to survive.

BENOIT (*di fuori*)
Si può?

MARCELLO
Chi è là?

BENOIT
Benoit.

MARCELLO
Il padrone di casa!

SCHAUNARD
Uscio sul muso.

COLLINE
Non c'è nessuno.

SCHAUNARD
È chiuso.

BENOIT
Una parola.

SCHAUNARD (*dopo essersi consultato cogli altri, va ad aprire*)
Sola!

Benoit enters.

BENOIT (*outside*)
May I come in?

MARCELLO
Who's there?

BENOIT
Benoit.

MARCELLO
The landlord!

SCHAUNARD
Bolt the door.

COLLINE
Nobody's home.

SCHAUNARD
It's locked.

BENOIT
Just one word.

SCHAUNARD (*after consulting the others, opens the door*)
Just one!

BENOIT *(mostrando una carta)*
Affitto.

BENOIT *(showing a paper)*
Rent.

MARCELLO
Olà! Date una sedia.

MARCELLO
Here! Give him a chair.

RODOLFO
Presto.

RODOLFO
At once.

BENOIT
Non occorre, lo vorrei…

BENOIT
Don't bother, I'd like…

SCHAUNARD
Segga.

SCHAUNARD
Be seated.

MARCELLO
Vuol bere?

MARCELLO
Something to drink?

BENOIT
Grazie.

BENOIT
Thank you.

RODOLFO E COLLINE
Tocchiamo.

RODOLFO AND COLLINE
A toast.

SCHAUNARD
Beva.

SCHAUNARD
Drink.

Benoit sets down his glass and shows the paper to Marcello.

BENOIT
Questo
è l'ultimo trimestre…

BENOIT
This is the bill
for three month's rent…

MARCELLO
E n'ho piacere…

MARCELLO
That's fine…

BENOIT	**BENOIT**
E quindi…	Therefore
SCHAUNARD	**SCHAUNARD**
Ancora un sorso.	Another drop.
BENOIT	**BENOIT**
Grazie.	Thank you.
I QUATTRO	**THE FOUR**
Tocchiam. Alla sua salute!	A toast. To your health!
BENOIT *(riprendendo con Marcello)*	**BENOIT** *(to Marcello again)*
A lei ne vengo	I come to you
perché il trimestre scorso	because last quarter
mi promise…	you promised me…
MARCELLO	**MARCELLO**
Promisi ed or mantengo.	I promised and I'll pay.
He points to the money on the table.	
RODOLFO *(piano a Marcello)*	**RODOLFO** *(aside to Marcello)*
Che fai?	What are you doing?
SCHAUNARD	**SCHAUNARD**
Sei pazzo?	Are you crazy?
MARCELLO *(a Benoit, senza guardare gli altri)*	**MARCELLO** *(to Benoit, ignoring the others)*
Ha visto? Or via,	You see? Now then
resti un momento in nostra compagnia.	stay with us a moment.
Dica quant'anni ha,	Tell me how old are you,
caro Signor Benoit?	dear M. Benoit?

BENOIT
Gli anni...Per carità!

RODOLFO
Su e giù la nostra età.

BENOIT
Di più, molto di più.

They refill his glass.

COLLINE
Ha detto su e giù.

MARCELLO
L'altra sera al Mabil
l'han colto in peccato d'amor.

BENOIT
Io?

MARCELLO
Al Mabil l'altra sera l'han colto...
Neghi?

BENOIT
Un caso.

MARCELLO
Bella donna!

BENOIT *(mezzo brillo)*
Ah! Molto!

SCHAUNARD POI RODOLFO
Briccone!

BENOIT
My age?...Spare me!

RODOLFO
Our age, more or less, I'd say.

BENOIT
More, much more.

COLLINE
He said more or less.

MARCELLO
The other evening at the Mabille
they caught him making love.

BENOIT
Me?

MARCELLO
They caught him at the Mabille the other
evening... Deny it, then.

BENOIT
An accident.

MARCELLO
A lovely woman!

BENOIT *(half-drunk)*
Ah! Very!

SCHAUNARD, THEN RODOLFO
You rascal!

COLLINE

Seduttore!

Una quercia…un cannone!

RODOLFO

L'uomo ha buon gusto.

MARCELLO

Il crin ricciuto e fulvo.

Ei gongolava arzillo e pettoruto.

BENOIT

Son vecchio ma robusto.

COLLINE, SCHAUNARD E RODOLFO

Ei gongolava arzuto e pettorillo.

MARCELLO

A lui cedea

la femminil virtù.

BENOIT

Timido in giovertù,

ora me ne ripago.

Si sa, è uno svago

qualche donnetta allegra…e…un po'…

non dico una balena

o un mappamondo

o un viso tondo da luna piena.

Ma magra, proprio magra, no, poi no!

Le donne magre son grattacapi

e spesso…sopracapi…

e son piene di doglie…

per esempio, mia moglie…

COLLINE

Seducer!

He's an oak, a ball of fire!

RODOLFO

He's a man of taste.

MARCELLO

With that curly, tawny hair.

How he swaggered, proud and happy!

BENOIT

I'm old but strong.

COLLINE, SCHAUNARD AND RODOLFO

How he swaggered, proud and happy!

MARCELLO

Feminine virtue

gave in to him.

BENOIT

I'm paying myself back now

for my shy youth…

my pastime, you know,

a lively woman…a bit…

well, not a whale exactly

or a relief-map of the world

or a face like a full moon,

but not thin, really thin. No!

Thin women are worrisome

and often…a nuisance…

always full of complaints,

for example—my wife! …

Marcello rises, feigning moral indignation. The others do the same.

MARCELLO
Quest'uomo ha moglie
e sconcie voglie ha nel cor!

GLI ALTRI
Orror!
RODOLFO
E ammorba, e appesta
la nostra onesta magion.

GLI ALTRI
Fuor!

MARCELLO
Si abbruci dello zucchero!

COLLINE
Si discacci il reprobo.

SCHAUNARD
È la morale offesa che vi scaccia!

BENOIT
Io di…io di…

GLI ALTRI
Silenzio!

BENOIT
Miei signori…

GLI ALTRI
Silenzio…via signore…
Via di qua! E buona sera
a vostra signoria! Ah! Ah! Ah!

MARCELLO
This man has a wife
and foul desires in his heart!

THE OTHERS
Horrors!
RODOLFO
He corrupts and pollutes
our respectable home.

THE OTHERS
Out with him!

MARCELLO
Burn some incense!

COLLINE
Throw out the scoundrel!

SCHAUNARD
Our offended morality expels you!

BENOIT
I say…I…

THE OTHERS
Silence!

BENOIT
My dear sirs…

THE OTHERS
Silence…Out, sir…
away with you! And good evening
to your worship! Ha! Ha! Ha!

Benoit is thrown out. Marcello shuts the door.

MARCELLO
Ho pagato il trimestre.

MARCELLO
I've paid the rent.

SCHAUNARD
Al Quartiere Latin ci attende Momus.

SCHAUNARD
In the Latin Quarter Momus awaits us.

MARCELLO
Viva chi spende!

MARCELLO
Long life to him who pays!

SCHAUNARD
Dividiamo il bottin!

SCHAUNARD
We'll divide my loot!

GLI ALTRI
Dividiam!

THE OTHERS
Let's divide!
They share the coins.

They share the coins.

MARCELLO *(presentando uno specchio a Colline)*
Là ci son beltà scese dal cielo.
Or che sei ricco, bada alla decenza!
Orso, ravviati il pelo.

MARCELLO *(giving Colline a mirror)*
Beauties are there, come from above.
Now you're rich, you must look presentable. You bear!
Trim your fur.

COLLINE
Farò la conoscenza
la prima volta d'un barbitonsore.
Guidatemi ai ridicolo
oltraggio d'un rasoio.

COLLINE
I'll make my first acquaintance
of a beard-barber.
Lead me to the absurd,
outrageous razor.

TUTTI
Andiam.

ALL
Let's go.

The violin plays a languid recollection of the theme we heard at the beginning of the opera, when it represented Rodolfo and his boisterous nature. Now it sounds as if the same man needs to be alone and find inspirations. Colline's fall down the stairs (00:37) draws our attention offstage, an area that will shortly assume new importance.

RODOLFO	**RODOLFO**
Io resto per terminar	I must stay to finish
l'articolo di fondo	my article for the paper,
del Castoro.	*The Beaver.*
MARCELLO	**MARCELLO**
Fa presto.	Hurry, then!
RODOLFO	**RODOLFO**
Cinque minuti. Conosco il mestier.	Five minutes. I know my trade.
COLLINE	**COLLINE**
T'aspetterem dabbasso dal portier.	We'll wait for you downstairs.
MARCELLO	**MARCELLO**
Se tardi udrai che coro.	You'll hear us if you dawdle.
RODOLFO	**RODOLFO**
Cinque minuti.	Five minutes.
SCHAUNARD	**SCHAUNARD**
Taglia corta la coda al tuo Castoro.	Cut that *Beaver's* tail short.

Rodolfo takes a light and opens the door. The others start down the stairs.

MARCELLO *(di fuori)*	**MARCELLO** *(outside)*
Occhio alla scala	Watch the stairs.
Tienti alla ringhiera	Hold on to the railing.

RODOLFO (*alzando il lume*)
Adagio.

COLLINE
È buio pesto.

SCHAUNARD
Maledetto portier!

COLLINE
Accidenti!

RODOLFO
Colline, sei morto?

COLLINE (*dal basso*)
Non ancor.

MARCELLO
Vien presto.

RODOLFO (*raising the light*)
Careful.

COLLINE
It's pitch dark.

SCHAUNARD
That damn janitor!

COLLINE
Hell!

RODOLFO
Colline, are you killed?

COLLINE (*from below*)
Not yet.

MARCELLO
Come soon.

Rodolfo closes the door, sets his light on the table, and tries to write. But he tears up the paper and throws the pen down.

RODOLFO
Non sono in vena.

RODOLFO
I'm not in the mood.

There's a timid knock at the door.

DISC NO. 1/TRACK 6

Mimì is heard before she is seen, a device Puccini uses in other operas as well for his heroines. It is an instruction to the audience, inviting us to "see" her primarily through our ears. The rest of this first section of their meetings is all short, broken phrases. The unspoken text is what counts in this initial encounter.

Chi è là?

MIMÌ *(di fuori)*
Scusi.

RODOLFO
Una donna!

MIMÌ
Di grazia, mi si è spento
il lume.

RODOLFO *(aprendo)*
Ecco.

MIMÌ *(sull'uscio, con un lume spento in mano ed una chiave)*
Vorrebbe…?

RODOLFO
S'accomodi un momento.

MIMÌ
Non occorre.

RODOLFO
La prego, entri.

Mimì enters, and has a fit of coughing.

Si sente male?

MIMÌ
No…nulla.

Who's there?

MIMÌ *(outside)*
Excuse me.

RODOLFO
A woman!

MIMÌ
I'm sorry…my light
has gone out.

RODOLFO *(opening the door)*
Here.

MIMÌ *(in the doorway, holding a candlestick and key)*
Would you…?

RODOLFO
Come in for a moment.

MIMÌ
There's no need.

RODOLFO
Please…come in.

You're not well?

MIMÌ
No…it's nothing.

RODOLFO

Impallidisce!

RODOLFO

You're pale!

MIMÌ

È il respir…quelle scale…

MIMÌ

I'm out of breath…the stairs…

She faints, and Rodolfo is just in time to support her and help her to a chair. The key and the candlestick fall from her hands.

RODOLFO

Ed ora come faccio?

RODOLFO

Now what shall I do?

He gets some water and sprinkles her face.

Così.
Che viso d'ammalata!

So.
How ill she looks!

Mimì comes to.

Si sente meglio?

Are you better now?

MIMÌ

Sì.

MIMÌ

Yes.

RODOLFO

Qui c'è tanto freddo
Segga vicino al fuoco.

RODOLFO

It's so cold here. Come and sit
by the fire.

He helps her to a chair by the stove.

Aspetti…un po' di vino.

Wait…some wine.

MIMÌ

Grazie.

MIMÌ

Thank you.

RODOLFO

A lei.

MIMÌ

Poco, poco.

RODOLFO

Così.

MIMÌ

Grazie.

RODOLFO

(Che bella bambina!)

MIMÌ *(alzandosi)*

Ora permetta
che accenda il lume.
Tutto è passato.

RODOLFO

Tanta fretta!

MIMÌ

Sì.

Rodolfo lights her candle for her.

Grazie. Buona sera.

RODOLFO

Buona sera.

Mimì goes out, then reappears at the door.

RODOLFO

Here.

MIMÌ

Just a little.

RODOLFO

There.

MIMÌ

Thank you.

RODOLFO

(What a lovely creature!)

MIMÌ *(rising)*

Now, please,
relight my candle.
I'm better now.

RODOLFO

Such a hurry!

MIMÌ

Yes.

Thank you. Good evening.

RODOLFO

Good evening.

Mimì returs to the music of Rodolfo's theme. Perhaps she is "in" on a type of game she is playing with Rodolfo, or perhaps we are to understand that he has found his inspiration at last.

MIMÌ
Oh! sventata, sventata!
la chiave della stanza
dove l'ho lasciata?

MIMÌ
Oh! foolish me!
Where have I left the key to my room?

RODOLFO
Non stia sull'uscio
il lume vacillá al vento.

RODOLFO
Don't stand in the door
the wind makes your light flicker.

Her candle goes out.

MIMÌ
Oh Dio! Torni ad accenderlo.

MIMÌ
Heavens! Will you relight it?

Rodolfo hastens to her with his light, but when he reaches the door, his candle goes out, too. The room is dark.

RODOLFO
Oh Dio! Anche il mio s'è spento.

RODOLFO
There…Now mine's out, too.

MIMÌ
Ah! E la chiave ove sarà?

MIMÌ
Ah! And where can my key be?

RODOLFO
Buio pesto!

RODOLFO
Pitch dark!

MIMÌ
Disgraziata!

MIMÌ
Unlucky me!

RODOLFO
Ove sarà?

RODOLFO
Where can it be?

MIMÌ

Importuna è la vicina…

RODOLFO

Ma le pare!

MIMÌ

Importuna è la vicina…

RODOLFO

Cosa dice? ma le pare!

MIMÌ

Cerchi.

RODOLFO

Cerco.

They hunt, touching the floor with their hands.

MIMÌ

Ove sarà?

RODOLFO

Ah!

He finds the key and pockets it.

MIMÌ

L'ha trovata?

RODOLFO

No.

MIMÌ

Mi parve…

MIMÌ

You've a bothersome neighbor…

RODOLFO

Not at all.

MIMÌ

You've a bothersome neighbor…

RODOLFO

What do you mean? Not at all!

MIMÌ

Search.

RODOLFO

I'm searching.

MIMÌ

Where can it be?

RODOLFO

Ah!

MIMÌ

Did you find it?

RODOLFO

No.

MIMÌ

I thought…

RODOLFO

In verità!

RODOLFO

Truthfully!

MIMÌ

Cerca?

MIMÌ

Are you hunting?

RODOLFO

Cerco.

RODOLFO

I'm hunting for it.

Guided by her voice, Rodolfo pretends to search as he draws closer to her. Then his hand meets hers, and he holds it.

MIMÌ *(sopresa)*

Ah!

MIMÌ *(surprised)*

Ah!

They rise. Rodolfo continues to hold Mimì's hand.

Rodolfo (Richard Tucker) and Mimì (Nadine Conner) discover they have fallen in love at first sight.

Che gelida manina **The first aria is sung when Rodolfo and Mimì are alone and he conspires to touch her hand. A shiver of delight that sets off a chain of extraordinary musical events, it is well worth the wait. Rodolfo's aria is possibly the most charming seduction in all of opera. After his transparent ploy to persuade Mimì to stay, he tells her in an expansive and swaggering turn of melody (01:24) that he is a poet richer than a millionaire because of his passion. But he also admits, in a more ardent melody (02:24), that he is already madly in love with her. He describes this rush of feeling as being like the dawn and giving him the sweetest hope. At this point, the tenor must rise to a high C. Many tenors routinely transpose the aria down a half tone, and Puccini himself reluctantly endorsed the idea when no less than Caruso (always wary of his high C) begged him to.**

RODOLFO	RODOLFO
Che gelida manina!	How cold your little hand is!
Se la lasci riscaldar.	Let me warm it for you.
Cercar che giova?	What's the use of searching?
Al buio non si trova.	We'll never find it in the dark.
Ma per fortuna	But luckily
è una notte di luna,	there's a moon,
e qui la luna l'abbiamo vicina.	and she's our neighbor here.
Aspetti, signorina,	Just wait, my dear young lady,
le dirò con due parole chi son,	and meanwhile I'll tell you
chi son, e che faccio, come vivo.	in a word who and what I am.
Vuole?	Shall I?

Mimì is silent.

Chi son? Chi son? Son un poeta.	Who am I? I'm a poet.
Che cosa faccio? Scrivo.	My business? Writing.
E come vivo? Vivo.	How do I live? I live.
In povertà mia lieta	In my happy poverty
scialo da gran signore	I squander like a prince
rime ed inni d'amore.	my poems and songs of love.
Per sogni e per chimere	In hopes and dreams
e per castelli in aria	and castles-in-air,

l'anima ho milionaria.	I'm a millionaire in spirit.
Talor dal mio forziere	But sometimes my strong-box
ruban tutti i gioielli	is robbed of all its jewels
due ladri gli occhi belli.	by two thieves; a pair of pretty eyes.
V'entrar con voi pur ora	They came in now with you
ed i miei sogni usati,	and all my lovely dreams,
ed i bei sogni miei	my dreams of the past,
tosto si dileguar!	were soon stolen away.
Ma il furto non m'accora	But the theft doesn't upset me,
poichè, poichè v'ha preso stanza	since the empty place was filled
la speranza.	with hope.
Or che mi conoscete	Now that you know me,
parlate voi. Deh parlate.	it's your turn to speak.
Chi siete? Vi piaccia dir?	Who are you? Will you tell me?

DISC NO. 1 / TRACK 9

Sì. Mi chiamono Mimì Mimì's response is as multifaceted as Rodolfo's. She begins halt-ingly, describing her humble existence in a melody of touching vulnerability. She is so modest that she asks Rodolfo if he is listening; he is, of course, hanging on her every word (01:42). When she resumes, she has a bit more confidence, detailing her day-to-day

Linda Ronstadt as Mimì and Gary Morris as Rodolfo in a New York Shakespeare Festival production of *La Bohème*.

life in the winter with a sprightly tune that changes only when she savors the image of spring. Suddenly, unable to contain her passion, Mimì extols the beauties of spring and its promise of love in an expansive, soaring melody (02:42) that reveals a robust soul quite different from the tubercular girl who knocked on the door and now, almost apologetically, emerges from her sudden reverie (04:40), apologizing for the intrusion.

MIMÌ
Sì.
Mi chiamano Mimì,
ma il mio nome è Lucia.
La storia mia è breve.
A tela o a seta
ricamo in casa e fuori.
Son tranquilla e lieta,
ed è mio svago
far gigli e rose.
Mi piaccion quelle cose
che han sì dolce malia,
che parlano d'amor, di primavere,
che parlano di sogni e di chimere,
quelle cose che han nome poesia…
Lei m'intende?

RODOLFO
Sì.

MIMÌ
Mi chiamano Mimì.
Il perchè non so.
Sola, mi fo il pranzo
da me stessa.
Non vado sempre a messa,
ma prego assai il Signor.
Vivo sola, soletta,
là in una bianca cameretta;

MIMÌ
Yes.
They call me Mimì,
but my real name's Lucia.
My story is brief.
I embroider silk and satin
at home or outside.
I'm tranquil and happy
and my pastime
is making lilies and roses.
I love all things
that have gentle magic,
that talk of love, of spring,
that talk of dreams and fancies—
the things called poetry…
do you understand me?

RODOLFO
Yes.

MIMÌ
They call me Mimì,
I don't know why.
I live by myself
and I eat alone.
I don't often go to church,
but I like to pray.
I stay all alone
in my tiny white room,

guardo sui tetti e in cielo.	I look at the roofs and the sky.
Ma quando vien lo sgelo	But when spring comes
il primo sole è mio,	the sun's first rays are mine.
il primo bacio dell'aprile è mio!	April's first kiss is mine, is mine!
Il primo sole è mio.	The sun's first rays are mine!
Germoglia in un vaso una rosa,	A rose blossoms in my vase,
foglia a foglia l'aspiro.	I breathe its perfume, petal by petal.
Così gentil è il profumo d'un fior.	So sweet is the flower's perfume.
Ma i fior ch'io faccio, ahimè,	But the flowers I make, alas,
i fior ch'io faccio,	the flowers I make, alas,
ahimè non hanno odore.	alas, have no scent.
Altro di me non le saprei narrare.	What else can I say?
Sono la sua vicina	I'm your neighbor, disturbing you
che la vien fuori d'ora a importunate.	at this impossible hour.

DISC NO. 1/TRACK 10

Puccini cleverly has the voices of the friends appear offstage, as if on the street below, creating an ensemble that informs the rest of the scene with additional melody, despite the distinctly intimate nature of the moment.

SCHAUNARD *(dal cortile)*	**SCHAUNARD** *(from below)*
Ehi! Rodolfo!	Hey! Rodolfo!
COLLINE	**COLLINE**
Rodolfo!	Rodolfo!
MARCELLO	**MARCELLO**
Olà! Non senti?	Hey! Can't you hear?
Lumaca!	You slow-coach!
COLLINE	**COLLINE**
Poetucolo!	You scribbler!

SCHAUNARD

Accidenti al pigro!

Rodolfo, impatient, goes to the window to answer. When the window is opened, the moonlight comes in, lighting up the room.

RODOLFO

Scrivo ancora tre righi a volo.

MIMÌ

Chi sono?

RODOLFO

Amici.

SCHAUNARD

Sentirai le tue.

MARCELLO

Che te ne fai lì solo?

RODOLFO

Non son solo. Siamo in due.
Andate da Momus, tenete il posto.
Ci saremo tosto.

**MARCELLO, SCHAUNARD
E COLLINE**

Momus, Momus, Momus,
zitti e discreti andiamocene via.
Momus, Momus.
Trovò la poesia.

SCHAUNARD

To hell with that lazy one!

RODOLFO

I've a few more words to write.

MIMÌ

Who are they?

RODOLFO

Friends.

SCHAUNARD

You'll hear about this.

MARCELLO

What are you doing there alone?

RODOLFO

I'm not alone. There's two of us.
Go to Momus and get a table.
We'll be there soon.

**MARCELLO, SCHAUNARD
AND COLLINE**

Momus, Momus, Momus.
Quietly, discreetly, we're off.
Momus, Momus.
He's found his poem at last.

Turning, Rodolfo sees Mimì wrapped in a halo of moonlight. He contemplates her, in ecstasy.

Café Momus in Rolf Gerard's stageset for a 1952-53 production at the Metropolitan Opera.

DISC NO. 1/TRACK 11

O soave fanciulla This rapturous duet captures the infatuation Rodolfo feels for Mimì—just seeing her standing in a shaft of moonlight mesmerizes him. Her feelings are the same. The duet climaxes quickly (00:39), but it is the afterglow that is so charming, as they banter about what might happen when they return from the Café Momus (02:36). Puccini sends them out into the night (03:19), deliriously happy, singing of love as their voices fade into the cold Christmas Eve air.

RODOLFO

O soave fanciulia, o dolce viso,
di mite circonfuso alba lunar,
in te ravviso il sogno
ch'io vorrei sempre sognar!

RODOLFO

Oh! lovely girl! Oh, sweet face
bathed in the soft moonlight.
I see in you the dream
I'd dream forever!

MIMÌ

(Ah, tu sol comandi, amor!…)

RODOLFO

Fremon già nell'anima
le dolcezze estreme.

MIMÌ

(Tu sol comandi, amore!)

RODOLFO

Fremon nell'anima
dolcezze estreme, ecc.
Nel bacio freme amor!

MIMÌ

(Oh! come dolci scendono
le sue lusinghe al core…
Tu sol comandi, amor!)

Rodolfo kisses her.

No, per pietà!

RODOLFO

Sei mia!

MIMÌ

V'aspettan gli amici…

RODOLFO

Già mi mandi via?

MIMÌ

Vorrei dir…ma non oso.

MIMÌ

(Ah! Love, you rule alone!…)

RODOLFO

Already I taste in spirit
the heights of tenderness!

MIMÌ

(You rule alone, o Love!)

RODOLFO

Already I taste in spirit
the heights of tenderness!
Love trembles in our kiss!

MIMÌ

(How sweet his praises
enter my heart…
Love, you alone rule!)

No, please!

RODOLFO

You're mine!

MIMÌ

Your friends are waiting.

RODOLFO

You send me away already?

MIMÌ

I daren't say what I'd like…

RODOLFO
Di'.

MIMÌ
Se venissi con voi?

RODOLFO
Che? Mimì!
Sarebbe così dolce restar qui.
C'è freddo fuori.

MIMÌ
Vi starò vicina!

RODOLFO
E al ritorno?

MIMÌ
Curioso!

RODOLFO
Dammi il braccio, o mia piccina…

MIMÌ
Obbedisco, signor!

RODOLFO
Che m'ami…di'…

MIMÌ
Io t'amo.

RODOLFO E MIMÌ *(mentre escono)*
Amor! Amor! Amor!

RODOLFO
Tell me.

MIMÌ
If I came with you?

RODOLFO
What? Mimì!
It would be so fine to stay here.
Outside it's cold.

MIMÌ
I'd be near you!

RODOLFO
And when we come back?

MIMÌ
Who knows?

RODOLFO
Give me your arm, my dear…

MIMÌ
Your servant, sir…

RODOLFO
Tell me you love me!

MIMÌ
I love you.

RODOLFO AND MIMÌ *(as they go out)*
Beloved! My love! My love!

Act 2

IN THE LATIN QUARTER A square with shops of all kinds. On one side is the Café Momus. Mimì and Rodolfo move about with the crowd. Colline is nearby at a rag-woman's stand. Schaunard is buying a pipe and a trumpet. Marcello is pushed here and there by the throng. It is evening. Christmas Eve.

DISC NO. 1/TRACK 12

Even the librettists tried to persuade Puccini that it would be illogical for the bohemians to spend the evening outdoors after they complained of the cold, but Puccini stood fast. The result was this magnificent view of the crowd dynamics, so detailed and complex that the initial audiences were completely baffled by it. Paris itself becomes an important character in the opera, yet we never lose the melodic thread of the principals in this most intimate of stories.

I VENDITORI	HAWKERS
Aranci, datteri!	Oranges, dates!
Caldi i marroni.	Hot roasted chestnuts!
Ninnoli, croci.	Crosses, knick-knacks!
Torroni e caramelle.	Cookies and candies!
Fiori alle belle.	Flowers for the ladies!
Oh! la crostata.	Pies for sale!
Panna montata.	With whipped cream!
Fringuelli, passeri.	Finches and larks!
Datteri! Trote!	Dates! Fresh fish!
Latte di cocco! Giubbe!	Coconut milk! Skirts!
Carote!	Carrots!

LA FOLLA	THE CROWD
Quanta folla! Che chiasso!	What a throng! Such noise!
Stringiti a me, corriamo.	Hold tight! Let's run!
Lisa! Emma!	Lisa! Emma!
Date il passo.	Make way there!
Emma, quando ti chiamo!	Emma, I'm calling you!
Ancora un altro giro…	Once more around…
Pigliam via Mazzarino.	We'll take Rue Mazarin,
Qui mi manca il respiro!…	I can't breathe here…
Vedi? Il Caffè è vicino.	See? The café's right here.
Oh! stupendi gioielli!	What wonderful jewels!
Son gli occhi assai più belli!	Your eyes are more wonderful!
Pericolosi esempi	This crowd tonight
la folla oggi ci dà!	sets a dangerous example!
Era meglio ai miei tempi!	Things were better in my day!
Viva la libertà!	Long live freedom!

At the Café

Andiam. Qua, camerier!	Let's go. Here, waiter!
Presto. Corri.	Hurry. On the run.
Vien qua. A me.	Come here. My turn.
Birra! Un bicchier!	Beer! A glass!
Vaniglia. Ratafià.	Vanilla. Liqueur!
Dunque? Presto!	Well? Hurry.
Da ber! Un caffè…	Drinks! Coffee…
Presto. Olà…	Quickly. Hey, there…

SCHAUNARD   **SCHAUNARD**

blowing on the trumpet, producing odd sounds

Falso questio Re!	This D is out of tune.
Pipa e corno quant'è?	How much for the horn and pipe?

COLLINE

at the rag-woman's, who is sewing up an enormous overcoat he has just bought

È un poco usato…

RODOLFO
Andiam.

MIMÌ
Andiam per la cuffietta?

COLLINE
Ma è serio e a buon mercato…

RODOLFO
Tienti al mio braccio stretta…

MIMÌ
A te mi stringo.

MIMÌ, RODOLFO
Andiam!

They go into the milliner's.

MARCELLO
Io pur mi sento in vena di grida:
Chi vuol, donnine allegre, un po' d'amor?

VENDITORI
Datteri! Trote! Prugne di Tours!

MARCELLO
Facciamo insieme a vendere e comprar:
Io do ad un soldo il vergine mio cuor.

COLLINE

It's a little worn…

RODOLFO
Let's go.

MIMÌ
Are we going to buy the bonnet?

COLLINE
…But it's cheap and dignified.

RODOLFO
Hold tight to my arm.

MIMÌ
I'll hold you tight.

MIMÌ, RODOLFO
Let's go!

MARCELLO
I, too, feel like shouting:
which of you happy girls wants love?

HAWKERS
Dates! Trout! Plums from Tours!

MARCELLO
Let us make a bargain together—
for a penny I'll sell my virgin heart.

SCHAUNARD
Fra spintoni e pestate accorrendo,
affretta la folla e si diletta
nel provar voglie matte—
insoddisfatte.

VENDITORI
Ninnoli, spillette! *ecc.*

COLLINE *(mostrando un libro)*
Copia rara, anzi unica
la grammatica Runica.

SCHAUNARD
(Uomo onesto!)

MARCELLO
A cena!

SCHAUNARD E COLLINE
Rodolfo?

MARCELLO
Entrò da una modista.

Rodolfo and Mimì come out of the shop.

RODOLFO
Vieni, gli amici aspettano.

MIMÌ
Mi sta ben questa cuffietta rosa?

VENDITORI
Panna montata! Latte di cocco!
Oh! la crostata! Panna montata!

SCHAUNARD
Pushing and shoving and running, the
crowd hastens to its joys,
feeling insane desires—
unappeased.

HAWKERS
Trinkets! Brooches! *etc.*

COLLINE *(showing a book)*
A rare find, truly unique
a Runic grammar.

SCHAUNARD
(What an honest fellow!)

MARCELLO
Let's eat!

SCHAUNARD AND COLLINE
And Rodolfo?

MARCELLO
He went into the milliner's.

RODOLFO
Come, my friends are waiting.

MIMÌ
Is my pink bonnet becoming?

HAWKERS
Whipped cream! Coconut milk!
Pies! Whipped cream!

AL CAFFÈ
Camerier! Un bicchier!
Presto Olà…Ratafia.

RODOLFO
Sei bruna
e quel color ti dona.

MIMÌ *(guardando verso la bottega)*
Bel vezzo di corallo.

RODOLFO
Ho uno zio milionario.
Se fa senno il buon Dio
voglio comprarti un vezzo
assai più bel!…

MONELLI, SARTINE, STUDENTI
Ah! ah! ah! ah! *ecc.*

BORGHESI
Facciam coda alla gente!
Ragazze, state attente!
Che chiasso! quanta folla!
Pigliam via Mazzarino!
Io soffoco, partiamo!
Vedi il caffè è vicin!
Andiam là, da Momus!
Ah!…

VENDITORI
Oh! la crostata! Panna montata!
Fiori alle belle!
Ninnoli, datteri, caldi i marron!
Fringuelli, passeri,
panna, torron!

CAFÈ CUSTOMERS
Waiter! A glass!
Quick. Hey there…Liqueur.

RODOLFO
You're dark,
that colour suits you.

MIMÌ *(looking back at the shop)*
That lovely coral necklace.

RODOLFO
I've a millionaire uncle.
If God acts wisely
I'll buy you a necklace
much more beautiful…

URCHINS, MIDINETTES, STUDENTS
Ah! ah! ah! *etc.*

TOWNSPEOPLE
Let's follow these people!
Girls, watch out!
Such noise! What a throng!
We'll take the Rue Mazarin!
I'm stifling, let's go!
See, the café's right here!
Let's go there, to Momus!
Ah!…

HAWKERS
Pies for sale! Whipped cream!
Flowers for the ladies!
Knick-knacks, dates, hot roasted chestnuts!
Finches, larks!
Cream cakes!

The friends interact with each other and with the crowd in ever more intriguing ways in this section. Note the overlap of the bohemians ordering expensive dishes at the café as the children whine for more toys (02:19). It's a sly comment that could only be made in opera, and only in the best operas.

RODOLFO
Chi guardi?

RODOLFO
Whom are you looking at?

COLLINE
Odio il profano volgo al par d'Orazio.

COLLINE
I hate the vulgar herd as Horace did.

MIMÌ
Sei geloso?

MIMÌ
Are you jealous?

RODOLFO
All'uom felice sta il sospetto
accanto.

RODOLFO
The man who's happy must be
suspicious too.

SCHAUNARD
Ed io quando mi sazio
vo' abbondanza di spazio.

SCHAUNARD
And when I'm stuffing myself
I want plenty of room about me.

MIMÌ
Sei felice?

MIMÌ
Are you happy then?

MARCELLO *(al cameriere)*
Vogliamo una cena prelibata.

MARCELLO *(to the waiter)*
We want a prize dinner.

RODOLFO
Ah, sì. Tanto.

RODOLFO
Oh yes. Very.

MARCELLO
Lesto.

MARCELLO
Quickly.

SCHAUNARD	**SCHAUNARD**
Per molti.	And bring plenty.
RODOLFO	**RODOLFO**
E tu?	And you?
MIMÌ	**MIMÌ**
Sì, tanto.	Very.

Marcello, Schaunard, and Colline sit at a table in front of the café.

STUDENTI	**STUDENTS**
Là, da Momus!	There, to Momus!
SARTINE	**MIDINETTES**
Andiam! Andiam!	Let's go! Let's go!
MARCELLO, COLLINE, SCHAUNARD	**MARCELLO, COLLINE, SCHAUNARD**
Lesto.	Quickly!
VOCE DI PARPIGNOL *(in lontananza)*	**VOICE OF PARPIGNOL** *(in the distance)*
Ecco i giocattoli di Parpignol!	Here are the toys of Parpignol!
RODOLFO	**RODOLFO**
Due posti!	Two places.
COLLINE	**COLLINE**
Finalmente, eccoci qui!	Here they are at last!
RODOLFO	**RODOLFO**
Questa è Mimì, gaia fioraia.	This is Mimì, happy flower-girl.
Il suo venir completa	Her presence alone
la bella compagnia.	makes our company complete.
Perché…perché son io il poeta;	For…for I am a poet;

essa la poesia.
Dal mio cervel sbocciano i canti,
dalle sue dita sbocciano i fior—
dall'anime esultanti
sboccia l'amor.

MARCELLO
Dio che concetti rari!

COLLINE
Digna est intrari.

SCHAUNARD
Ingrediat si necessit.

COLLINE
Io non do che un accessit.

VOCE DI PARPIGNOL *(più vicino)*
Ecco i giocattoli di Parpignol!

COLLINE
Salame…

Parpignol arrives in the square, pushing a barrow covered with frills and flowers.

RAGAZZI E BAMBINE
Parpignol! Parpignol! Parpignol!…
Ecco Parpignol! Parpignol!
Col carretto tutto fior!
Ecco Parpignol!
Voglio la tromba, il cavallin!
Il tambur, tamburel…
Voglio il cannon, voglio il frustin,
dei soldati i drappel.

and she is poetry itself.
As songs flow from my brain,
the flowers bloom in her hands,
and in joyful spirits
love blossoms also.

MARCELLO
What rare imagery!

COLLINE
Digna es intrari.

SCHAUNARD
Ingrediat si necessit.

COLLINE
I grant only one accessit.

VOICE OF PARPIGNOL *(closer)*
Here are the toys of Parpignol!

COLLINE
Salami…

CHILDREN
Parpignol! Parpignol! Parpignol!
Here is Parpignol!
With his cart all decked with flowers!
Here is Parpignol!
I want the horn, the toy horse!
The drum! The tambourine!
I want the cannon; I want the whip,
I want the troop of soldiers.

SCHAUNARD
Cervo arrosto.

MARCELLO
Un tacchino.

SCHAUNARD
Vin del Reno!

COLLINE
Vin da tavola!

SCHAUNARD
Aragosta senza crosta!

MAMME
Ah! che razza di furfanti indemoniati,
che ci venite a fare in questo loco?
A casa, a letto! Via, brutti sguaiati,
gli scappellotti vi parranno poco!…
A casa! A letto,
razza di furfanti, a letto!

UN RAGAZZO
Vo' la tromba, il cavallin…

RODOLFO
E tu Mimì, che vuoi?

MIMÌ
La crema.

SCHAUNARD
E gran sfarzo.
C'è una dama.

SCHAUNARD
Roast venison.

MARCELLO
A turkey.

SCHAUNARD
Rhine wine!

COLLINE
Table wine!

SCHAUNARD
Shelled lobster!

MOTHERS
What a bunch of naughty rascals!
What are you doing here now?
Go home to bed, you noisy things.
Slaps will be the least you'll get…
Go home to bed,
you bunch of rascals, to bed!

A BOY
I want the horn, the toy horse.…

RODOLFO
What will you have, Mimì?

MIMÌ
Some custard.

SCHAUNARD
The best.
A lady's with us.

RAGAZZI E BAMBINE	CHILDREN
Viva Parpignol!	Bravo Parpignol!
Il tambur, tamburel…	The drums! The tambourine!
Dei soldati il drappel.	A troop of soldiers!

DISC NO. 1/TRACK 14

The crowd fades into the backgroud as the friends concentrate on each other at the dinner table. Their intimacy is shortly invaded by the shrieking laughter of Musetta (02:09), bringing the crowd back into the score with her.

They run off, following Parpignol.

MARCELLO	MARCELLO
Signorina Mimì, che dono raro	Tell me, Mimì, what rare gift
le ha fatto il suo Rodolfo?	has Rodolfo given you?

MIMÌ	MIMÌ
Una cuffietta a pizzi tutta rosa	An embroidered pink bonnet, all
ricamata. Coi miei capelli bruni	with lace. It goes well
ben si fonde.	with my dark hair.
Da tanto tempo tal cuffietta	I've longed for such a bonnet
è cosa desiata…ed egli ha letto	for months….and he read
quel che il core asconde…	what was hidden in my heart…
Ora colui che legge dentro a un core	Anyone who can read the heart's secret
sa l'amore…ed è lettore.	knows love…he's such a reader.

SCHAUNARD	SCHAUNARD
Esperto professore…	He's a professor in the subject.

COLLINE	COLLINE
Che ha già diplomi e non son armi	With diplomas, and his verses
primele sue rime…	are not a beginner's…

SCHAUNARD

Tanto che sembra ver
ciò che egli esprime!

MARCELLO

O bella età d'inganni e d'utopie!
Si crede, spera, e tutto bello appare.

RODOLFO

La più divina delle poesie
è quella, amico, che c'insegna ad amare

MIMÌ

Amare è dolce ancora più del miele!

MARCELLO

Secondo il palato è miele o fiele!

MIMÌ

O Dio, l'ho offeso!

RODOLFO

È in lutto, o mia Mimì.

SCHAUNARD E COLLINE

Allegri! e un toast.

MARCELLO

Qua del liquor!

TUTTI

E via i pensier,
alti i bicchier. Beviam.

SCHAUNARD

That's why what he says
seems to be true!

MARCELLO

Oh, sweet age of false utopias!
You hope and believe, and all seems
beautiful.

RODOLFO

The poem most divine, my friend,
is what teaches us to love!

MIMÌ

Love is sweet, sweeter than honey.

MARCELLO

That depends it's honey or gali!

MIMÌ

Heavens! I've offended him!

RODOLFO

He's mourning, Mimì.

SCHAUNARD AND COLLINE

Cheer up! A toast!

MARCELLO

Something to drink!

ALL

Away with brooding,
raise you glass. We'll drink.

MARCELLO *(vedendo Musetta che entra, ridendo)*
Ch'io beva del tossico!

MARCELLO *(seeing Musetta enter, laughing)*
I'll drink some poison!

SCHAUNARD, COLLINE E RODOLFO
Oh! Musetta!

SCHAUNARD, COLLINE E RODOLFO
Oh! Musetta!

MARCELLO
Essa!

MARCELLO
Her!

LE BOTTEGAIE
To'! Lei! Sì! To'! Lei!
Musetta!
Siamo in auge! Che toeletta!

THE SHOPWOMEN
What! Her! Yes! Well! Her!
Musetta!
She's made it. What a dress!

Musetta stops, accompanied by the old and pompous Alcindoro. She sits at another table in front of the café.

ALCINDORO
Come un facchino
correr di qua…di là…
No, no, non ci sta…

ALCINDORO
Running like a porter
back and forth…
No, it's not proper.

MUSETTA *(chiamando Alcindoro come si chiama un cane)*
Vien, Lulù!

MUSETTA *(calling Alcindoro as if he were a dog)*
Here, Lulu!

ALCINDORO
Non ne posso più.

ALCINDORO
I can't take any more.

MUSETTA
Vien, Lulù.

MUSETTA
Come, Lulu.

SCHAUNARD
Quel brutto coso mi par che sudi!

SCHAUNARD
That ugly old fool all in a lather!

ALCINDORO	ALCINDORO
Come? qui fuori? qui?	What? Outside? Here?

MUSETTA	MUSETTA
Siedi. Lulù.	Sit, Lulu.

ALCINDORO	ALCINDORO
Tali nomignoli,	Please, save these
prego, serbateli	little nicknames of yours
al tu per tu.	for when we're alone.

MUSETTA	MUSETTA
Non farmi il Barbablù!	Don't act like Bluebeard!

COLLINE	COLLINE
È il vizio contegnoso…	He's evil behind that front!

MARCELLO	MARCELLO
Colla casta Susanna.	With the chaste Susanna.

MIMÌ	MIMÌ
Essa è pur ben vestita.	But she's beautifully dressed.

RODOLFO	RODOLFO
Gli angeli vanno nudi.	Angels go naked.

MIMÌ	MIMÌ
La conosci? Chi è?	You know her? Who is she?

DISC NO. 1/TRACK 15

Marcello decries the crimes of Musetta while she decides to win him back in what must be opera's most curious instance of a dyfunctional love duet. The comments of the others overlap and evanesce in a miracle of organic construction.

MARCELLO

Domandatelo a me.
Il suo nome è Musetta…
Cognome — Tentazione!
Per sua vocazione
fa la rosa dei venti;
gira e muta soventi
d'amanti e d'amore…
E come la civetta
è uccello sanguinario;
il suo cibo ordinario
è il cuore…mangia il cuore!
Per questo io non ne ho più.

MUSETTA

(Marcello è là…mi vide…
E non mi guarda il vile!
Quel Schaunard che ride!
Mi fan tutti una bile!
Se potessi picchiar,
se potessi graffiar!
Ma non ho sotto man
che questo pellican.
Aspetta!)
Ehi! Camerier!

MARCELLO *(nascondendo la commozione)*
Passatemi il ragù.

MUSETTA

Ehi! Camerier! questo piatto
ha una puzza di rifritto!

throwing the plate on the ground

MARCELLO

Ask me that question.
Her first name's Musetta.
Her last name's Temptation.
Her occupation is being
a leaf in the wind…
Always turning, changing
her lovers and her loves…
Like the screech-owl
she's a bird of prey.
Her favourite food
is the heart…she devours them!
And so I have no heart.

MUSETTA

(Marcello's there…he saw me…
But the coward won't look at me.
And that Schaunard's laughing!
They all make me livid!
If I could just hit them!
Scratch their eyes out!
But I've got this old
pelican on my hands.
Just wait!)
Waiter!

MARCELLO *(hiding his emotion)*
Pass me the stew.

MUSETTA

Hey! Waiter! This plate
smells dirty to me!

ALCINDORO
No, Musetta, zitto, zitto!

MUSETTA
(Non si volta.)

ALCINDORO
Zitto. Zitto. Modi. Garbo.

MUSETTA
(Ah! Non si volta.)

ALCINDORO
A chi parli?

COLLINE
Questo pollo è un poema!

MUSETTA
(Ora lo batto, lo batto!)

ALCINDORO
Con chi parli?

MUSETTA
Al cameriere. Non seccar!

SCHAUNARD
Il vino è prelibato!

MUSETTA
Voglio fare il mio piacere…

ALCINDORO
Parla pian!

ALCINDORO
No, Musetta! Quiet, now!

MUSETTA
(He won't look.)

ALCINDORO
Quiet, now. Manners! Please!

MUSETTA
(He won't look.)

ALCINDORO
To whom are you speaking?

COLLINE
This chicken is a poem!

MUSETTA
(Now I'll hit him, I'll hit him!)

ALCINDORO
Who are you talking to?

MUSETTA
To the waiter. Don't be a bore!

SCHAUNARD
The wine is excellent.

MUSETTA
I want my own way!

ALCINDORO
Lower your voice!

MUSETTA
Vo' far quel che mi pare!

ALCINDORO
Parla pian, parla pian!

MUSETTA
Non secc-a-a-ar!

SARTINE E STUDENTI
Guarda, guarda, chi si vede,
proprio lei, Musetta!
Con quel vecchio che balbetta,
proprio lei, Musetta!
Ah! ah! ah! ah!

MUSETTA
(Che sia geloso di questa mummia?)

ALCINDORO
La convenienza…il grado…la virtù!

MUSETTA
(Vediamo se mi resta
tanto poter su lui
da farlo cedere.)

SCHAUNARD
La commedia è stupenda!

MUSETTA (*guardando Marcello*)
Tu non mi guardi.

ALCINDORO
Vedi bene che ordino?

MUSETTA
I'll do as I please!

ALCINDORO
Lower your voice!

MUSETTA
Don't be a bore!

MIDINETTES AND STUDENTS
Look, look who it is,
Musetta herself!
With that stuttering old man,
it's Musetta herself!
Ha ha ha ha ha!

MUSETTA
(But could he be jealous of this mummy?)

ALCINDORO
Decorum…my rank…my reputation!

MUSETTA
(Let's see if I still
have enough power over him
to make him give in.)

SCHAUNARD
The play is stupendous!

MUSETTA (*looking at Marcello*)
You aren't looking at me.

ALCINDORO
Can't you see I'm ordering?

SCHAUNARD
La commedia è stupenda!

COLLINE
Stupenda!

RODOLFO *(a Mimì)*
Sappi per tuo governo
che non darei perdono in sempiterno.

SCHAUNARD
Essa all'un parla perché l'altro intenda.

MIMÌ *(a Rodolfo)*
Io t'amo tanto, e sono
tutta tua…
Che mi parli di perdono?

COLLINE *(a Schaunard)*
E l'altro invan crudel
finge di non capir,
ma sugge miel.

MUSETTA
Ma il tuo cuore martella.

ALCINDORO
Parla piano.

MUSETTA
Ma il tuo cuore martella.

ALCINDORO
Piano, piano!

SCHAUNARD
The play is stupendous!

COLLINE
Stupendous!

RODOLFO *(to Mimì)*
Let me tell you now
I'd never be forgiving.

SCHAUNARD
She speaks to one for the other to hear.

MIMÌ *(to Rodolfo)*
I love you so, and I'm
all yours…
Why speak of forgiveness?

COLLINE *(to Schaunard)*
And the other, cruel, in vain
pretends he is deaf,
but enjoys it all.

MUSETTA
But your heart's like a hammer.

ALCINDORO
Lower your voice.

MUSETTA
But your heart's like a hammer.

ALCINDORO
Lower your voice.

DISC NO. 1/TRACK 16

Quando men' vo The most famous melody from the score occurs in Act II. It is a teasing waltz melody sung by the self-absorbed Musetta, who marvels at the effect she has on people. The song seems to be aimed directly at Marcello who was once her lover. The tension between them becomes unbearable in the ensuing ensemble (02:20), and, when Musetta finally conspires to be with him, Marcello joyously reprises the melody of the waltz (03:43) as he waits to embrace her amid the madness of the moment.

MUSETTA	**MUSETTA**
Quando men' vo soletta	As I walk alone
per la via,	through the streets,
la gente sosta e mira,	the people stop to look
e la bellezza mia	and inspect my beauty,
tutta ricerca in me,	examining me
ricerca in me da capo a piè.	from head to toe.
MARCELLO	**MARCELLO**
Legatemi alla seggiola!	Tie me to the chair!
ALCINDORO	**ALCINDORO**
Quella gente che dirà?	What will people say?
MUSETTA	**MUSETTA**
Ed assaporo allor la bramosia	And then I savour the subtle
sottil che dagli occhi traspira	longing in their eyes
e dai palesi vezzi intender sa	when, from my visible charms,
alle occulte beltà.	they guess at the beauty concealed.
Così l'effluvio del desio	This onrush of desire
tutta m'aggira.	surrounds me.
Felice mi fa, felice mi fa.	It delights me, it delights me.
ALCINDORO	**ALCINDORO**
(Quel canto scurrile	(This scurrilous song
mi muove la bile!)	infuriates me!)

Frances Greer as Musetta in a 1944 production.

MUSETTA

E tu che sai, che memori e ti struggi,
da me tanto rifuggi?
So ben le angoscie tue
non le vuoi dir,
ma ti senti morir.

MIMÌ

Io vedo ben che quella poveretta
tutta invaghita di Marcello ell'è!

ALCINDORO

Quella gente che dirà?

MUSETTA

And you know, who remember and suffer,
how can you escape?
I know you won't admit
that you're in torment,
but it's killing you.

MIMÌ

I can tell that the poor girl
is head over heels in love with Marcello.

ALCINDORO

What will people say?

RODOLFO
Marcello un dì l'amò…

RODOLFO
Marcello loved her once…

SCHAUNARD
Ah! Marcello cederà!

SCHAUNARD
Ah! Marcello will give in!

RODOLFO
…La fraschetta l'abbandonò…

RODOLFO
…the flirt ran off…

COLLINE
Chi sa mai quel che avverrà!

COLLINE
Who knows what'll happen!

RODOLFO
…per poi darsi
a miglior vita.

RODOLFO
…to find
a better life.

SCHAUNARD
Trovan dolce a pari il laccio
chi lo tende e chi ci dà.

SCHAUNARD
The snare is equally sweet
to hunter and hunted.

COLLINE
Santi numi! in simil briga
mai Colline intopperà!

COLLINE
Gods above! I'd never land myself
in such a situation!

MUSETTA
(Ah! Marcello smania…
Marcello è vinto!)

MUSETTA
(Ah! Marcello's going mad!
Marcello is vanquished!)

ALCINDORO
Parla piano…Zitto, zitto!

ALCINDORO
Lower your voice! Be quiet!

MIMÌ
Quell'infelice mi muove a pietà.

MIMÌ
I feel so sorry for the poor girl.

COLLINE
Essa è bella — non son cieco…

MIMÌ *(stringendosi a Rodolfo)*
T'amo!

SCHAUNARD
(Quel bravaccio a momenti cederà!
Stupenda è la commedia!
Marcello cederà.)

to Colline

Se una tal vaga persona
ti trattasse a tu per tu,
la tua scienza brontolona
manderesti a Belzebù.

RODOLFO
Mimì!
È fiacco amore
quel che le offese vendicar no sa.
Spento amor non risorge, *ecc.*

MIMÌ
Quell'infelice mi muove a pietà.
L'amor ingeneroso è tristo amor!
Quell'infelice, *ecc.*

COLLINE
…ma piaccionmi assai più
una pipa e un testo greco.
Essa è bella, non son cieco, *ecc.*

ALCINDORO
Modi, garbo! Zitto, zitto!

COLLINE
She's lovely—I'm not blind…

MIMÌ *(nestling close to Rodolfo)*
I love you!

SCHAUNARD
(The braggart is about to yield!
The play is stupendous!
Marcello will give in!)

If such a pretty creature
stopped and talked to you,
you'd gladly send to the devil
all your bearish philosophy.

RODOLFO
Mimì!
Love is weak
when it leaves wrongs unavenged.
Love, once dead, cannot be revived, *etc.*

MIMÌ
I feel so sorry for the poor girl.
Love is sad when it's unforgiving.
I feel so sorry, *etc.*

COLLINE
…but I'm much happier
with my pipe and a Greek text.
She's beautiful, I'm not blind, *etc.*

ALCINDORO
Mind your manners! Be quiet!

109

MUSETTA

So ben le angoscie tue non le vuoi dir.
Ah! ma ti senti morir.

to Alcindoro

Io voglio fare il mio piacere,
voglio far quel che mi par.
Non seccar, non seccar, non seccar!
(Or conviene liberarsi del vecchio.)

pretending a pain

Ahi!

ALCINDORO

Che c'è?

MUSETTA

Qual dolore, qual bruciore!

ALCINDORO

Dove?

MUSETTA

Al piè!

MARCELLO

(Gioventù mia, tu non sei morta,
né di te è morto il sovvenir…
Se tu battessi alla mia porta
t'andrebbe il mio core ad aprir!)

MUSETTA

Sciogli! slaccia! rompi! straccia!
Te ne imploro.

MUSETTA

I know you won't admit your torment.
Ah! but you feel like dying!

I'll do as I please!
I'll do as I like,
don't be a bore, a bore, a bore!
(Now to get rid of the old man.)

Ouch!

ALCINDORO

What is it?

MUSETTA

The pain! The pain!

ALCINDORO

Where?

MUSETTA

My foot!

MARCELLO

(My youth, you're still alive,
your memory's not dead…
If you came to my door,
my heart would open it!)

MUSETTA

Loosen it! Untie it! Break it! Tear it!
Please!

Laggiù c'è un calzolaio.
Corri presto! ne voglio un altro paio.
Ahi! che fitta, maledetta scarpa stretta!
Or la levo...eccola qua.
Corri, va, corri! Presto, va, va!

MIMÌ
(Io vedo ben ell'è invaghita di Marcello.)

RODOLFO
(Io vedo ben la commedia è stupenda!)

ALCINDORO
Imprudente!
Quella gente che dirà?
Ma il mio grado!
Vuoi ch'io comprometta?
Aspetta! Musetta! Vo'!

He hurries off.

COLLINE E SCHAUNARD
(La commedia è stupenda!)

MUSETTA
Marcello!

MARCELLO
Sirena!

They embrace passionately.

SCHAUNARD
Siamo all'ultima scena!

The waiter brings the bill.

There's a shoemaker nearby.
Run quickly! I want another pair!
Ah, how it pinches, this damn tight shoe!
I'll take it off...here it is.
Run, go on, run! Hurry, hurry!

MIMÌ
(I can see she's madly in love with Marcello.)

RODOLFO
(I can see the play's stupendous!)

ALCINDORO
How unwise!
What will people say?
My reputation!
Do you want to ruin it?
Wait! Musetta! I'm going!

COLLINE AND SCHAUNARD
(The play is stupendous!)

MUSETTA
Marcello!

MARCELLO
Siren!

SCHAUNARD
Here's the finale!

TUTTI	ALL
Il conto!	The bill!

SCHAUNARD	SCHAUNARD
Così presto?	So soon?

COLLINE	COLLINE
Chi l'ha richiesto?	Who asked for it?

SCHAUNARD	SCHAUNARD
Vediam.	Let's see.

DISC NO. 1/TRACK 17

At the end of the act, the friends's whispering concerns about who will pay the bill are juxtaposed with the distant sounds of the marching band, which shortly overtakes all other music in the score. The friends literally "get lost" in the crowd around the band (01:22) as all Paris seems to celebrate the unions of the lovers.

COLLINE E RODOLFO	COLLINE AND RODOLFO
Caro!	It's high!

Drums are heard approaching.

RODOLFO, SCHAUNARD, COLLINE	RODOLFO, SCHAUNARD, COLLINE
Fuori il danaro!	Out with the money!

SCHAUNARD	SCHAUNARD
Colline, Rodolfo e tu, Marcel?	Colline, Rodolfo and you, Marcello?

MONELLI	CHILDREN
La Ritirata!	The Tattoo!

MARCELLO	MARCELLO
Siamo all'asciutto!	We're broke!

SCHAUNARD
Come?

SCHAUNARD
What?

SARTINE, STUDENTI
La Ritirata!

MIDINETTES, STUDENTS
The Tattoo!

RODOLFO
Ho trenta soldi in tutto!

RODOLFO
I've only got thirty sous.

BORGHESI
La Ritirata!

TOWNSPEOPLE
The Tattoo!

MARCELLO, SCHAUNARD, COLLINE
Come? Non ce n'è più?

MARCELLO, SCHAUNARD, COLLINE
What? No more money?

SCHAUNARD
Ma il mio tesoro ov'è?

SCHAUNARD
Where's my wealth?

MONELLI
S'avvicinan per di qua?

URCHINS
Are they coming this way?

MUSETTA *(al cameriere)*
Il mio conto date a me.

MUSETTA *(to the waiter)*
Bring me my bill.

SARTINE, STUDENTI
No! Di là!

MIDINETTES, STUDENTS
No! That way!

MONELLI
S'avvicinan per di là!

URCHINS
They're coming this way!

SARTINI, STUDENTI
Vien di qua!

MIDINETTES, STUDENTS
They're coming that way!

MONELLI
No! vien di là!

URCHINS
No, that way!

MUSETTA
Bene!

BORGHESI, VENDITORI
Largo! largo!

RAGAZZI
Voglio veder! voglio sentir!

MUSETTA
Presto, sommate quello con questo!…
Paga il signor che stava qui con me.

MAMME
Lisetta, vuoi tacere?
Tonio, la vuoi finire?

FANCIULLE
Mamma, voglio vedere!
Papà, voglio sentìre!

**RODOLFO, MARCELLO,
SCHAUNARD, COLLINE**
Paga il signor!

RAGAZZI
Vuò veder la Ritirata!

MAMME
Vuoi tacer, la vuoi finir!

SARTINE
S'avvicinano di qua!

BORGHESI
S'avvicinano di là!

MUSETTA
Good!

TOWNSPEOPLE
Make way! Make way!

CHILDREN
I want to see! I want to hear!

MUSETTA
Quick, add these two bills together…
The gentleman who was with me will pay.

MOTHERS
Lisetta, please be quiet.
Tonio, stop that at once!

GIRLS
Mama, I want to see.
Papa, I want to hear.

**RODOLFO, MARCELLO,
SCHAUNARD, COLLINE**
The gentleman will pay!

CHILDREN
I want to see the Tattoo!

MOTHERS
Please be quiet! Stop that at once!

MIDINETTES
They're coming this way!

TOWNSPEOPLE
They're coming that way!

BORGHESI, STUDENTI, VENDITORI
Sì, di qua!

MONELLI
Come sarà arrivata,
la seguiremo al passo.

COLLINE, SCHAUNARD, MARCELLO
Paga il signor!

MUSETTA
E dove s'è seduto,
ritrovi il mio saluto!

putting the bill on the chair

BORGHESI
In quel rullìo tu senti
la patria maestà.

**RODOLFO, COLLINE,
SCHAUNARD, MARCELLO**
E dove s'è seduto,
ritrovi il suo saluto!

LA FOLLA
Largo, largo, eccoli qua!

MONELLI
Ohè attenti, eccoli qua!

MARCELLO
Giunge la Ritirata!

LA FOLLA
In fila!

TOWNSPEOPLE, STUDENTS, HAWKERS
Yes, this way!

URCHINS
When it comes by,
we'll march with it!

COLLINE, SCHAUNARD, MARCELLO
The gentleman will pay!

MUSETTA
And here, at his place,
he'll find my farewell!
putting the bill on the chair

TOWNSPEOPLE
That drum-roll expresses
our country's glory.

**RODOLFO, COLLINE,
SCHAUNARD, MARCELLO**
And here, at this place,
he'll find her farewell!

THE CROWD
Make way, make way, here they come!

URCHINS
Hey! Look out, here they are!

MARCELLO
Now the Guard is coming!

THE CROWD
All in line!

COLLINE, MARCELLO
Che il vecchio non ci veda
fuggir colla sua preda.

RODOLFO
Giunge la Ritirata!

MARCELLO, SCHAUNARD, COLLINE
Quella folla serrata
il nascondiglio appresti!

LA FOLLA
Ecco il tambur maggiore, più fiero
d'un antico guerriero! Il tambur maggior!

MIMÌ, MUSETTA, RODOLFO,
MARCELLO, SCHAUNARD, COLLINE
Lesti! lesti! lesti!

LA FOLLA
I Zappatori! i Zappatori, olà!
Ecco il tambur maggior!
Pare un general!
La Ritirata è qua!
Eccola là Il bel tambur maggior!
La canna d'or, tutto splendor!
Che guarda, passa, va!

RODOLFO, MARCELLO,
SCHAUNARD, COLLINE
Viva Musetta! Cuor biricchin!
Gloria ed onor, onor e gloria
del Quartier Latin!

COLLINE, MARCELLO
Don't let the old fool see us
make off with his prize.

RODOLFO
The Guard is coming!

MARCELLO, SCHAUNARD, COLLINE
That crowded throng
will be our hiding-place.

THE CROWD
Here's the drum-major! Produer
than an ancient warrior! The drum-major!

MIMÌ, MUSETTA, RODOLFO,
MARCELLO, SCHAUNARD, COLLINE
Hurry! Let's run off!

THE CROWD
The Sappers! The Sappers, hooray!
Here's the drum-major!
Like a general!
The Tattoo is here!
Here he is, the handsome drum-major!
The golden baton, all a-glitter!
See, he looks at us as he goes past!

RODOLFO, MARCELLO,
SCHAUNARD, COLLINE
Bravo Musetta! Artful minx!
Glory and honour, the glory and honour
of the Latin Quarter!

LA FOLLA	**THE CROWD**
Tutto splendor!	All a-glitter!
Di Francia è il più bell'uom!	The handsomest man in France,
Il bel tambur maggior!	the drum-major!
Eccola là Che guarda, passa, va!	Here he is! See, he looks at us as he goes past!

Since Musetta cannot walk with only one shoe, Marcello and Colline carry her on their shoulders. They all follow the guards and disappear. Alcindoro comes back with a new pair of shoes, and the waiter hands him the bill. When he sees the amount and sees nobody around, Alcindoro falls, bewildered, onto a chair.

Act II in a 1991 production by the Houston Grand Opera.

Act 3

THE BARRIÈRE D'ENFER Beyond the tollgate is the main highway. At left, a tavern. A small square flanked by plane trees. Some customs officers are asleep around a brazier. Shouts and laughter issue from the cabaret. Dawn. February. The snow is everywhere. Some street-sweepers are beyond the gate, stamping their feet in the cold.

DISC NO. 2/TRACKS 1 & 2

The brash exuberance of Act 2 now devolves into the pathos of this sad, snowbound act. The contrast is explicit in the very melancholy orchestral introduction of falling chords, a superb musical analogy of the frozen landscape. Listen again: it's actually the theme Schaunard had sung when describing the joys of the Latin Quarter, which was played in its fullest form at the beginning of Act 2. Here, it is three times as slow as it had been previously, like the painful recollection of a happy time while in misery.

SPAZZINI	**SWEEPERS**
Ohè là, le guardie…Aprite!	Hey, there! Guards! Open up!
Quelli di Gentilly! Siam gli spazzini,	We're the sweepers from Gentilly.
Fiocca la neve. Ohè, là! Qui s'agghiaccia.	It's snowing. Hey! We're freezing here.
UN DOGANIERE *(sbadigliando)*	**CUSTOMS OFFICER** *(yawning)*
Vengo.	I'm coming.
VOCI DAL CABARET	**VOICES FROM THE TAVERN**
Chi nel ber trovò il piacer	Some find pleasure
nel suo bicchier,	in their cups.
d'una bocca nell'ardor	On ardent lips
trovò l'amor.	some find love.

VOCE DI MUSETTA	**VOICE OF MUSETTA**
Ah! Se nel bicchier sta il piacer,	Ah! Pleasure is in the glass!
il giovin bocca sta l'amor	Love lies on your lips.
VOCI DAL CABARET	**VOICES FROM THE TAVERN**
Trallerallè	Tar la la la
Eva e Noè.	Eve and Noah.
VOCI DAL BOULEVARD	**VOICES FROM THE HIGHWAY**
Hopp-là! Hopp-là!	Houp-la! Giddap!
DOGANIERE	**CUSTOMS OFFICER**
Son già le lattivendole!	Here come the milkmaids!

He opens the gate. The milkmaids enter together with a string of peasants' carts.

LE LATTIVENDOLE	**MILKMAIDS**
Buon giorno!	Good morning!
LE CONTADINE	**PEASANT WOMEN**
Burro e cacio!	Butter and cheese!
Polli ed ova!	Chickens and eggs!
Voi da che parte andate?	Which way are you going?
A San Michele.	To Saint Michel!
Chi troverem più tardi?	Shall we meet later?
A mezzodi.	Yes, at noon.

They go off. Enter Mimì. When she reaches the first tree, she has a fit of coughing. Then recovering herself, she says to the sergeant

MIMÌ	**MIMÌ**
Sa dirmi, scusi, qual è	Excuse me, where's the tavern
l'osteria dove un pittor lavora?	where a painter is working?
SERGENTE	**SERGEANT**
Eccola.	There it is.

MIMÌ	**MIMÌ**
Grazie.	Thank you.

A waitress comes out of the tavern. Mimì approaches her.

O buona donna, mi fate il favore	Oh, good woman, please…
di cercarmi il pittore	Be good enough to find me
Marcello? Ho da parlargli.	Marcello, the painter.
Ho tanta fretta.	I must see him quickly.
Ditegli, piano, che Mimì l'aspetta.	Tell him Mimì's waiting.

SERGENTE *(ad uno che passa)*	**SERGEANT** *(to someone coming in)*
Ehi, quel paniere!	Hey! That basket!

DOGANIERE	**CUSTOMS OFFICER**
Vuoto!	Empty!

SERGENTE	**SERGEANT**
Passi.	Let him through.

Marcello comes out of the tavern.

DISC NO. 2/TRACK 3

Mimì, though almost breathless when she arrives, pours out her emotions to Marcello, doubled by the orchestra (00:53). This is a technique used by "verismo" composers to tell us of a character's unadorned, unedited sincerity.

MARCELLO	**MARCELLO**
Mimì?!	Mimì?!

MIMÌ	**MIMÌ**
Speravo di trovarvi qui.	I hoped I'd find you here.

MARCELLO

È ver, siam qui da un mese
di quell'oste alle spese.
Musetta insegna il canto
ai passeggieri.
Io pingo quei guerrieri
sulla facciata.
È freddo. Entrate.

MIMÌ

C'è Rodolfo?

MARCELLO

Sì.

MIMÌ

Non posso entrar.
No! No!

MARCELLO

Perché?

MIMÌ

O buon Marcello, aiuto! Aiuto!

MARCELLO

Cos'è avvenuto?

MIMÌ

Rodolfo m'ama e mi fugge
Rodolfo si strugge per gelosia.
Un passo, un detto, un vezzo,
un fior lo mettono in sospetto…
Onde corrucci ed ire.
Talor la notte fingo di dormire

MARCELLO

That's right. We've been here
a month, at the host's expense.
Musetta teaches
the guests singing.
And I paint those warriors
by the door there.
It's cold. Come inside.

MIMÌ

Is Rodolfo there?

MARCELLO

Yes.

MIMÌ

I can't go in.
No, no!

MARCELLO

Why not?

MIMÌ

Oh! help me, good Marcello! Help me!

MARCELLO

What's happened?

MIMÌ

Rodolfo—he loves me
but flees from me, torn
by jealousy. A glance, a gesture,
a smile, a flower arouses
his suspicions, then anger, rage…
Sometimes at night I pretend

e in me lo sento fisso
spiarmi i sogni in viso.
Mi grida ad ogni istante
non fai per me, ti prendi
un altro amante,
non fai per me. Ahimè!
In lui parla il rovello, lo so;
ma che rispondergli, Marcello?

MARCELLO
Quando s'è come voi
non si vive in compagnia.

MIMÌ
Dite bene. Lasciarci conviene.
Aiutateci, aiutateci voi.
Noi s'è provato
più volte, ma invano.

MARCELLO
Son lieve a Musetta,
ella è lieve a me,
perché ci amiamo in allegria.
Canti e risa, ecco il fior
d'invariabile amor!

MIMÌ
Dite bene, dite bene.
Lasciarci conviene.
Fate voi per il meglio.

MARCELLO
Sta ben. Ora lo sveglio.

MIMÌ
Dorme?

to sleep, and I feel his eyes
trying to spy on my dreams.
He shouts at me all the time
"You're not for me.
Find another.
You're not for me." Alas!
I know it's his jealousy speaking,
but what can I answer, Marcello?

MARCELLO
When two people are like you two,
they can't live together.

MIMÌ
You're right. We should separate.
Help us, Marcello, help us.
We've tried
again and again, but in vain.

MARCELLO
I take Musetta lightly,
and she behaves like me.
We love light-heartedly.
Laughter and song—that's the secret
of a lasting love.

MIMÌ
You're right, you're right.
We should separate.
Do your best for us.

MARCELLO
All right. I'll wake him up.

MIMÌ
Is he sleeping?

MARCELLO
È piombato qui
un'ora avanti l'alba.
S'assopì sopra una panca.
Guardate.

Mimì coughs.

Che tosse!

MIMÌ
Da ieri ho l'ossa rotte.
Fuggì da me stanotte
dicendomi è finita.
A giorno sono uscita
e me ne venni a questa volta.

MARCELLO *(osservando Rodolfo
nell'interno)*
Si desta…s'alza.
Mi cerca. Viene.

MIMÌ
Ch'ei non mi veda.

MARCELLO
Or rincasate, Mimì.
Per carità, non fate scene qua!

Mimì hides behind a tree, Rodolfo hastens out of the tavern.

MARCELLO
He stumbled in here
an hour before dawn
and fell asleep on a bench.
Look at him…

What a cough!

MIMÌ
I've been aching all over since
yesterday. He fled during the night, saying
"It's all over." I set out
at dawn and came here to find you.

MARCELLO *(watching Rodolfo through
the window)*
He's waking up. He's looking
for me…Here he comes.

MIMÌ
He mustn't see me.

MARCELLO
Go home now, Mimì.
For God's sake, no scenes here.

Rodolfo hides his true emotions in macho posturing, which is something tenors convey better than anyone. Marcello, of course, see through it all.

RODOLFO	**RODOLFO**
Marcello. Finalmente.	Marcello. At last!
Qui niun ci sente.	No one can hear us here.
Io voglio separarmi da Mimì.	I've got to leave Mimì.
MARCELLO	**MARCELLO**
Sei volubil così?	Are you as fickle as that?
RODOLFO	**RODOLFO**
Già un'altra volta credetti	Already once before I thought
morto il mio cor.	my heart was dead.
Ma di quegli occhi azzurri	But it revived at the gleam
allo splendor esso è risorto.	of her blue eyes.
Ora il tedio l'assale…	Now boredom assails it…
MARCELLO	**MARCELLO**
E gli vuoi rinnovare il funeral?	And you'll bury it again?
RODOLFO	**RODOLFO**
Per sempre!	Forever!
MARCELLO	**MARCELLO**
Cambia metro.	Change your ways!
Dei pazzi è l'amor tetro	Gloomy love is madness
che lacrime distilla	and brews only tears.
Se non ride e sfavilla,	If it doesn't laugh and glow
l'amore è fiacco e roco.	love has no strength or voice.
Tu sei geloso.	You're jealous.
RODOLFO	**RODOLFO**
Un poco.	A little.

MARCELLO

Collerico, lunatico,
imbevuto di pregiudizi,
noioso, cocciuto!

MIMÌ

(Or lo fa incollerire!
Me poveretta!)

RODOLFO

Mimì è una civetta
che frascheggia con tutti.
Un moscardino di Viscontino
le fa l'occhio di triglia.
Ella sgonnella e scopre la caviglia
con un far promettente e lusinghier.

MARCELLO

Lo devo dir?
Che non mi sembri sincer.

RODOLFO

Ebbene, no. Non lo son.
Invan, invan nascondo
la mia vera tortura.
Amo Mimì sovra ogni cosa
al mondo. Io l'amo! Ma ho paura.

MARCELLO

You're raving mad,
a mass of suspicions,
a boor, a mule!

MIMÌ

(He'll make him angry.
Poor me!)

RODOLFO

Mimì's just a flirt
toying with them all.
A foppish Viscount eyes her
with longing. She shows him
her ankles, promising,
luring him on.

MARCELLO

Must I tell you?
You aren't being honest.

RODOLFO

All right, then, I'm not.
I try in vain to hide
what really torments me.
I love Mimì more than the world.
I love her! But I'm afraid…

DISC NO. 2/TRACK 6

This celebrated trio reveals Rodolfo's true motivations at last as Mimì confronts the reality of her situation. The melody (00:22) seems like the musical analog of repressed sobs.

Mimì è tanto malata!
Ogni dì più declina.
La povera piccina
è condannata…

Mimì is terribly ill,
weaker every day.
The poor little thing
is doomed…

MARCELLO

Mimì?

MIMÌ

(Che vuoi dire?)

RODOLFO

Una terribil tosse
l'esil petto le scuote.
Già la smunte gote
di sangue ha rosse…

MARCELLO

Povera Mimì!

MIMÌ

(Ahimè, morire?)

RODOLFO

La mia stanza è una tana
squallida. Il fuoco è spento.
V'entra e l'aggira il vento
di tramontana.
Essa canta e sorride
e il rimorso m'assale.
Me, cagion del fatale
mal che l'uccide.

MARCELLO

Che far dunque?

MIMÌ

(O mia vita! È finita!
Ahimè! morir! *ecc.*)

MARCELLO

Mimì?

MIMÌ

(What does he mean?)

RODOLFO

A horrible coughing
racks her fragile chest…
Her pale cheeks
are flushed…

MARCELLO

Poor Mimì!

MIMÌ

(Am I dying? Alas!)

RODOLFO

My room's like a cave.
The fire has gone out.
The wind, the winter wind
roars through it.
She laughs and sings;
I'm seized with remorse.
I'm the cause of the illness
that's killing her.

MARCELLO

What's to be done?

MIMÌ

(Oh! my life! It's over!
Alas! To die! *etc.*)

RODOLFO

Mimì di serra è fiore.
Povertà l'ha sfiorita,
per richiamarla in vita
non basta amore.

MARCELLO

Poveretta. Povera Mimì! Povera Mimì!

Mimì sobs and coughs.

RODOLFO

Che! Mimì! Tu qui!
M'hai sentito?

MARCELLO

Ella dunque ascoltava.

RODOLFO

Facile alla paura,
per nulla io m'arrovello.
Vien là nel tepore.

He tries to lead her inside.

MIMÌ

No, quel tanfo mi soffoca.

Musetta's laughter comes from inside.

RODOLFO

Ah! Mimì!

MARCELLO

È Musetta che ride.

RODOLFO

Mimì's a hothouse flower,
blighted by poverty.
To bring her back to life
love's not enough.

MARCELLO

Poor thing. Poor Mimì!

RODOLFO

What, Mimì? You here!
You heard me?

MARCELLO

She was listening then.

RODOLFO

I'm easily frightened,
worked up over nothing.
Come inside where it's warm.

MIMÌ

No. It's so close. I'd suffocate.

RODOLFO

Ah, Mimì!

MARCELLO

That's Musetta laughing.

| Con chi ride? | And with whom? |
| Ah la civetta! Imparerai. | The flirt! I'll teach her. |

Marcello runs into the tavern.

Addio … D'onde lieta uscì al tuo grido Mimì's aria of farewell comes after she, from a hiding place, has overheard Rodolfo telling Marcello that she is mortally ill, and that his jealousy and frustration are driven by the idea that he might lose her. A coughing fit reveals to the men that she has been listening, and when Rodolfo tries to explain himself she tells him she must leave him. She bids him farewell in a lyrical moment equal to her first-act aria. Beginning with a halting tenderness and gathering the strength that blossoms into melody (02:23), she says she will have someone pick up her things, though he might want to keep the little bonnet he bought her the night they met.

Beniamino Gigli
(1890-1957) as Rodolfo.

MIMÌ *(a Rodolfo)*	**MIMÌ** *(to Rodolfo)*
Addio.	Good-bye.

RODOLFO	**RODOLFO**
Che! Vai?	What? You're going?

MIMÌ	**MIMÌ**
D'onde lieta uscì al tuo grido	Back to the place I left
d'amore torna sola Mimì.	at the call of your love.
Al solitario nido	I'm going back alone
ritorna un'altra volta	to my lonely nest
a intesser finti fior.	to make false flowers.
Addio senza rancor.	Good-bye…no hard feelings.
— Ascolta, ascolta.	But listen.
Le poche robe aduna che lasciai	Please gather up the few things
sparse. Nel mio cassetto	I've left behind. In the trunk
stan chiusi quel cerchietto	there's the little bracelet
d'or e il libro di preghiere.	and my prayer book. Wrap them…
Involgi tutto quanto in un grembiale	in an apron and I'll send
e manderò il portiere…	someone for them…
— Bada, sotto il guanciale	wait! Under my pillow
c'è la cuffietta rosa.	there's my pink bonnet.
Se vuoi…serbarla a ricordo d'amor…	If you want…keep it in memory
Addio, senza rancor.	of our love. Good-bye, no hard feelings.

DISC NO. 2/TRACK 8

Dunque è proprio finita Immediately following Mimì's farewell, this scene, which emerges as a quartet, proves the third act is the heart and soul of La Bohème. It fills out superbly the characters of Mimì, Rodolfo, Musetta, and Marcello, with Puccini's wonderfully reflexive writing catching the tensions and transforming them into expressive melody (01:05). The tragic mood and the sweetness of the music is contrasted by the amusing bickering of Musetta and Marcello (01:57), reminding the listener that life rattles on for most people, even as Mimì and Rodolfo contemplate a different future.

RODOLFO

Dunque è proprio finita.

Te ne vai, la mia piccina?

Addio, sogni d'amor!

MIMÌ

Addio dolce svegliare alla mattina.

RODOLFO

Addio sognante vita!

MIMÌ

Addio rabuffi e gelosie…

RODOLFO

…Che un tuo sorriso acqueta.

MIMÌ

Addio sospetti…

RODOLFO

So it's really over.

You're leaving, my little one?

Good-bye to our dreams of love.

MIMÌ

Good-bye to our sweet wakening.

RODOLFO

Good-bye, life in a dream.

MIMÌ

Good-bye, doubts and jealousies…

RODOLFO

That one smile of yours could dispel.

MIMÌ

Good-bye, suspicions…

RODOLFO

Baci.

MIMÌ

…Pungenti amarezze…

RODOLFO

…Ch'io da vero poeta
rimavo con carezze.

RODOLFO E MIMÌ

Soli, l'inverno è cosa da morire!

MIMÌ

Soli…

RODOLFO E MIMÌ

Mentre a primavera
c'è compagno il sol.

MIMÌ

C'è compagno il sol.

Marcello and Musetta come out, quarreling.

MARCELLO

Che facevi? Che dicevi?
Presso il foco a quel signore?

MUSETTA

Che vuoi dir? Che vuoi dir?

MIMÌ

Niuno è solo l'april.

RODOLFO

Kisses…

MIMÌ

…Poignant bitterness…

RODOLFO

…That, like a poet,
I made rhyme with caress.

RODOLFO AND MIMÌ

To be alone in winter is death!

MIMÌ

Alone…

RODOLFO AND MIMÌ

But when spring comes
the sun is our companion.

MIMÌ

The sun is our companion.

MARCELLO

What were you doing and saying
by the fire with that man?

MUSETTA

What do you mean? What do you mean?

MIMÌ

Nobody's lonely in April.

MARCELLO

Al mio venire
hai mutato di colore.

MUSETTA

Quel signore mi diceva…
"Ama il ballo, signorina?"

RODOLFO

Si parla coi gigli e le rose.

MIMÌ

Esce dai nidi un cinguettìo gentile.

MARCELLO

Vana, frivola civetta!

MUSETTA

Arrossendo io rispendevo
"Ballerei sera e mattina."

MARCELLO

Quel discorso asconde mire
disoneste.

MUSETTA

Voglio piena libertà.

MARCELLO

Io t'acconcio per le feste…

RODOLFO E MIMÌ

Al fiorir di primavera
c'è compagno il sol.

MARCELLO

When I came in
you blushed suddenly.

MUSETTA

The man was asking me…
"Do you like dancing, Miss?"

RODOLFO

One can speak to roses with lilies.

MIMÌ

Birds twitter softly in their nests.

MARCELLO

Vain, empty-headed flirt!

MUSETTA

I blushed and answered
"I could dance day and night!"

MARCELLO

That speech conceals
infamous desires.

MUSETTA

I want complete freedom.

MARCELLO

I'll teach you a thing or two…

RODOLFO AND MIMÌ

With the coming of spring,
the sun is our companion!

MUSETTA

Che mi canti?
Che mi gridi? Che mi canti?
All'altar non siamo uniti.

MARCELLO

…Se ti colgo a incivettire!
Bada, sotto il mio cappello
non ci stan certi ornamenti.

MUSETTA

Io detesto quegli amanti
che la fanno da mariti.

RODOLFO E MIMÌ

Chiacchieran le fontane,
la brezza della sera balsami
stende sulle doglie umane.

MARCELLO

Io non faccio da zimbello
ai novizi intraprendenti.
Vana, frivola civetta!
Ve ne andate? Vi ringrazio,
or son ricco divenuto.

MUSETTA

Fo all'amor chi mi piace.
Non ti garba?
Fo all'amor con chi mi piace.
Musetta se ne va.

MARCELLO E MUSETTA

Vi saluto.

MUSETTA

What do you think
you're saying?
We're not married, after all.

MARCELLO

…If I catch you flirting!
Keep in mind, no horns
will grow under my hat.

MUSETTA

I can't stand lovers
who act just like husbands.

RODOLFO AND MIMÌ

The fountains whisper,
the evening breeze heals the pain
of human creatures…

MARCELLO

I won't be laughed at
by some young upstart.
Vain, empty-headed flirt!
You're leaving? I thank you,
I'll be a rich man then.

MUSETTA

I'll flirt with whom I please.
You don't like it?
I'll flirt with whom I please.
Musetta goes her way.

MARCELLO AND MUSETTA

Good-bye.

RODOLFO E MIMÌ
Vuoi che aspettiam
la primavera ancor?

MUSETTA
Signor, addio
vi dico con piacer!

MARCELLO
Son servo e me ne vo!

MUSETTA *(mentre ella se ne va)*
Pittore da bottega!

MARCELLO
Vipera!

MUSETTA
Rospo!

MARCELLO *(ritornando nella taverna)*
Strega!

MIMÌ
Sempre tua…per la vita.

RODOLFO E MIMÌ
Ci lascieremo alla stagion dei fior!

MIMÌ
Vorrei che eterno
durasse il verno!

RODOLFO E MIMÌ
Ci lascierem alla stagion dei fior!

RODOLFO AND MIMÌ
Shall we wait
until spring comes again?

MUSETTA
I bid you, sir,
farewell—with pleasure!

MARCELLO
Your servant, and I'm off!

MUSETTA *(leaving)*
You house-painter!

MARCELLO
Viper!

MUSETTA
Toad!

MARCELLO *(re-entering the tavern)*
Witch!

MIMÌ
Always yours.…all my life.

RODOLFO AND MIMÌ
We'll part when the flowers bloom!

MIMÌ
I wish that winter
would last forever!

RODOLFO AND MIMÌ
We'll part when flowers bloom!

Act 4

THE GARRET Marcello once more at his easel; Rodolfo at his table. They try to work, but instead they are talking.

DISC NO. 2/TRACK 9

In un coupè? **The fourth act begins just as the first act did, with the theme of the bohemians Puccini borrowed from his *Capriccio sinfonico*. It is slightly altered, suggesting change and the passage of time, and it lands the listener squarely in the middle of an idle conversation in which Rodolfo recounts to Marcello how and where he had seen Musetta recently.**

MARCELLO	**MARCELLO**
In un coupè?	In a coupé?
RODOLFO	**RODOLFO**
Con pariglia e livree.	With footmen and horses.
Mi salutò ridendo.	She greeted me, laughing.
Tò Musetta — le dissi —	"So, Musetta," I said,
e il cuor?	"your heart?
"Non batte o non lo sento	It doesn't beat—at least I don't feel it.
grazie al velluto che il copre."	Thanks to the velvet that covers it."
MARCELLO	**MARCELLO**
Ci ho gusto davver.	I'm glad, really glad.
RODOLFO	**RODOLFO**
(Loiola va. Ti rodi e ridi.)	(Faker, go on! You're laughing
	and fretting inside.)

MARCELLO

Non batte? Bene.

Io pur vidi…

RODOLFO

Musetta?

MARCELLO

Mimì.

RODOLFO

L'hai vista?

with pretended unconcern

Oh guarda!

MARCELLO

Era in carrozza

vestita come una regina.

RODOLFO

Evviva. Ne son contento.

MARCELLO

(Bugiardo. Si strugge d'amor.)

RODOLFO

Lavoriam.

MARCELLO

Lavoriam.

MARCELLO

Not beating? Good.

I also saw…

RODOLFO

Musetta?

MARCELLO

Mimì.

RODOLFO

You saw her?

Really?

MARCELLO

She was in a carriage

dressed like a queen.

RODOLFO

That's fine. I'm delighted.

MARCELLO

(The liar! Love's consuming him.)

RODOLFO

Let's get to work.

MARCELLO

Yes, to work.

They start working, but quickly throw down brush and pen.

RODOLFO

Che penna infame!

MARCELLO

Che infame pennello!

RODOLFO

This pen is terrible!

MARCELLO

So is this brush!

DISC NO. 2/TRACK 10

Ah, Mimì, tu più non torni **The idle gossip makes both men wistful, and each longs to see his beloved again. The duet they sing is richly sentimental, full of regret tinged with a little hope (01:41). But after a bit of swagger from both singers, they are left with nothing else to say (or sing), and—as they ponder their memories (02:28)—it is up to the orchestra to finish the melody.**

RODOLFO

(O Mimì, tu più non torni.
O giorni belli,
piccole mani, odorosi capelli,
collo di neve! Ah! Mimì,
mia breve gioventù.)

MARCELLO

(Io non so come sia
che il mio pennello lavori
e impasti colori contro voglia mia.
Se pingere mi piace
o cielo o terre
o inverni o primavere,
egli mi traccia due pupille nere
e una bocca procace,
e n'esce di Musetta il viso ancor…

RODOLFO

(E tu, cuffietta lieve,
che sotto il guancial partendo

RODOLFO

(O Mimì, you won't return!
O lovely days! Those tiny hands,
those sweet-smelling locks,
that snowy neck! Ah! Mimì!
My short-lived youth.)

MARCELLO

(I don't understand how my brush
works and mixes colours
to spite me.
Whether I want to paint
earth or sky, spring
or winter, the brush
outlines two dark eyes
and inviting lips,
and Musetta's face comes out…)

RODOLFO

(And you, little pink bonnet
that she hid under the pillow

137

ascose, tutta sai	as she left, you know
la nostra felicità,	all of our joy.
vien sul mio cor,	Come to my heart,
sul mio cor morto,	my heart that's dead
poiché è morto amor.)	with our dead love.)

MARCELLO

(E n'esce di Musetta il viso
tutto vezzi e tutto frode.
Musetta intanto gode
e il mio cuor vile
la chiama ed aspetta.)

MARCELLO

(Her face comes forward then,
so lovely and so false.
Meanwhile Musetta is happy
and my cowardly heart
calls her, and waits for her.)

DISC NO. 2/TRACKS 11 & 12

This final act is in many ways a reflection of the first act, except that everything has changed for the friends. Schaunard returns to the garret with only a herring, and the subsequent gaiety has a forced quality that was absent from the first act. Even a silly minuet in cheap drag abruptly turns into a mock-fight (track 12, 00:46).

RODOLFO

Che ora sia?

RODOLFO

What time is it?

MARCELLO

L'ora del pranzo…
Di ieri.

MARCELLO

It's time for dinner…
yesterday's dinner.

RODOLFO

E Schaunard non torna.

RODOLFO

And Schaunard's not back.

Schaunard comes in and sets four rolls on the table. Colline is with him.

SCHAUNARD

Eccoci.

SCHAUNARD

Here we are.

RODOLFO E MARCELLO	**RODOLFO AND MARCELLO**
Ebbene?	Well?
MARCELLO	**MARCELLO**
Del pan?	Just bread?
COLLINE	**COLLINE**
È un piatto degno di Demostene	A dish worthy of Demosthenes
un'aringa…	A herring…
SCHAUNARD	**SCHAUNARD**
…salata.	…salted.
COLLINE	**COLLINE**
Il pranzo è in tavola. *(Si seggono.)*	Dinner's on the table. *(They sit down.)*
MARCELLO	**MARCELLO**
Questa è cuccagna	This is like a feast day
da Berlingaccio.	in wonderland.
SCHAUNARD *(Mette la bottiglia*	**SCHAUNARD** *(puts the water-bottle in*
d'acqua nel cappello di Colline)	*Colline's hat)*
Ora lo sciampagna	Now let's put
mettiamo in ghiaccio.	the champagne on ice.
RODOLFO	**RODOLFO**
Scelga, o Barone,	Which do you choose, Baron,
trota o salmone?	salmon or trout?
MARCELLO	**MARCELLO**
Duca, una lingua	Well, Duke, how about
di pappagallo?	some parrot-tongue?
SCHAUNARD	**SCHAUNARD**
Grazie, m'impingua,	Thanks, but it's fattening.
stasera ho un ballo.	I must dance this evening.

Colline gets up.

RODOLFO
Già sazio?

COLLINE
Ho fretta.
Il Re m'aspetta.

MARCELLO
C'è qualche trama?

**RODOLFO, MARCELLO,
SCHAUNARD**
Qualche mister?

COLLINE
Il Re mi chiama
al minister.

**MARCELLO, RODOLFO,
SCHAUNARD**
Bene!

COLLINE
Però vedrò…Guizot!

SCHAUNARD
Porgimi il nappo.

MARCELLO
Sì. Bevi. Io pappo.

SCHAUNARD
Mi sia permesso…
al nobile consesso…

RODOLFO
Full already?

COLLINE
I'm in a hurry.
The King is waiting for me.

MARCELLO
Is there some plot?

**RODOLFO, MARCELLO,
SCHAUNARD**
Some mystery?

COLLINE
The King has asked me
to join his cabinet.

**MARCELLO, RODOLFO,
SCHAUNARD**
Fine!

COLLINE
So…I'll see Guizot!

SCHAUNARD
Pass me the goblet.

MARCELLO
Here. Drink. I'll eat.

SCHAUNARD
By the leave…
of this noble company…

RODOLFO
Basta.

MARCELLO
Fiacco!

COLLINE
Che decotto!

MARCELLO
Leva il tacco.

COLLINE
Dammi il gotto.

SCHAUNARD
M'ispira irresistibile
l'estro della romanza…

GLI ALTRI
No!

SCHAUNARD
Azione coreografica allora?

GLI ALTRI
Sì.

SCHAUNARD
La danza con musica vocale!

COLLINE
Si sgombrino le sale.
Gavotta.

RODOLFO
Enough!

MARCELLO
Weakling!

COLLINE
What a concoction!

MARCELLO
Get out of here!

COLLINE
The goblet, please.

SCHAUNARD
I'm irresistibly inspired
by the Muse of poetry…

THE OTHERS
No!

SCHAUNARD
Something choreographic then?

THE OTHERS
Yes.

SCHAUNARD
Dance with vocal accompaniment!

COLLINE
Let the hall be cleared.
A gavotte.

MARCELLO
Minuetto.

RODOLFO
Pavanella.

SCHAUNARD
Fandango.

COLLINE
Propongo la quadriglia.

RODOLFO
Mano alle dame.

COLLINE
Io detto.

SCHAUNARD
La lera la lera la!

RODOLFO *(galante a Marcello)*
Vezzosa damigella…

MARCELLO
Rispetti la modestia.
La prego.

COLLINE
Balancez.

SCHAUNARD
Prima c'è il Rond.

MARCELLO
Minuet.

RODOLFO
Pavane.

SCHAUNARD
Fandango.

COLLINE
I suggest the quadrille.

RODOLFO
Take your lady's arm.

COLLINE
I'll call the figures.

SCHAUNARD
La lera la lera la!

RODOLFO *(gallantly, to Marcello)*
Lovely maiden…

MARCELLO
Please, sir,
respect my modesty.

COLLINE
Balancez.

SCHAUNARD
The Rond comes first.

COLLINE

No, bestia.

SCHAUNARD

Che modi da lacchè!

COLLINE

Se non erro lei m'oltraggia.

Snudi il ferro.

SCHAUNARD

Pronti. Assaggia.

Il tuo sangue voglio ber.

Colline takes the fire-tongs and Schaunard the poker. They fight as the others sing.

COLLINE

Un di noi si sbudella.

SCHAUNARD

Apprestate una barella.

COLLINE

Apprestate un cimiter.

RODOLFO E MARCELLO

Mentre incalza la tenzone

gira e balza Rigodone.

Musetta enters

MARCELLO

Musetta!

COLLINE

No, damn it.

SCHAUNARD

What boorish manners!

COLLINE

You provoke me, I believe.

Draw your sword.

SCHAUNARD

Ready. Lay on.

I'll drink your blood.

COLLINE

One of us will be run through!

SCHAUNARD

Have a stretcher ready!

COLLINE

And a graveyard too!

RODOLFO AND MARCELLO

While the battle rages,

the dancers circle and leap.

MARCELLO

Musetta!

C'è Mimì … c'è Mimì **The cavorting of the young men stops suddenly, sickeningly, when Musetta arrives with the news that she has the desperately ill Mimì downstairs with nowhere else to turn. The household suddenly mobilizes on her behalf. As demonstrated in the first act, Puccini is unparalleled in his ability to capture this kind of activity, down to the smallest detail, in a smooth flow of musical ideas.**

MUSETTA	**MUSETTA**
C'è Mimì…c'è Mimì	Mimì's here…she's coming
che mi segue e che sta male.	and she's ill.
RODOLFO	**RODOLFO**
Ov'è?	Where is she?
MUSETTA	**MUSETTA**
Nel far le scale	She couldn't find strength
più non si resse.	to climb all the stairs.

Rodolfo hastens out to Mimì, who is seated on the last step. Then they carry her into the room and place her on the bed.

RODOLFO	**RODOLFO**
Ah!	Ah!
SCHAUNARD	**SCHAUNARD**
Noi accostiamo quel lettuccio.	We'll move the bed closer.
RODOLFO	**RODOLFO**
Là. Da bere.	Here. Something to drink.
MIMÌ	**MIMÌ**
Rodolfo.	Rodolfo.
RODOLFO	**RODOLFO**
Zitta. Risposa.	Rest now. Don't speak.

MIMÌ

O mio Rodolfo,
mi vuoi qui con te?

RODOLFO

Ah, mia Mimì!
Sempre, sempre!

MUSETTA *(agli altri, piano)*

Intesi dire che Mimì, fuggita
dal Viscontino, era in fin di vita.
Dove stia? Cerca, cerca…la veggo
passar per via,
trascinandosi a stento
Mi dice, "Più non reggo…
Muoio, lo sento…
Voglio morir con lui…
Forse m'aspetta…"

MARCELLO

Sst!

MIMÌ

Mi sento assai meglio…

MUSETTA

"…M'accompagni, Musetta?"

MIMÌ

Lascia ch'io guardi intorno.
Ah, come si sta bene qui.
Si rinasce, si rinasce…
Ancor sento la vita qui…
No, tu non mi lasci più…

MIMÌ

O my Rodolfo!
You want me here with you?

RODOLFO

Ah! My Mimì!
Always, always!

MUSETTA *(aside, to the others)*

I heard Mimì had fled
from the Viscount and was dying.
Where was she? I sought her…
Just now I saw her in the street
stumbling along. She said,
"I can't last long.
I know I'm dying…
but I want to die with him…
Perhaps he's waiting for me.."

MARCELLO

Sh!

MIMÌ

I feel much better…

MUSETTA

"…Please take me, Musetta?"

MIMÌ

Let me look around.
How wonderful it is here.
I'll recover… I will…
I feel life here again.
You won't leave me ever…

RODOLFO
Benedetta bocca,
tu ancor mi parli.

MUSETTA
Che ci avete in casa?

MARCELLO
Nulla.

MUSETTA
Non caffè? Non vino?

MARCELLO
Nulla. Ah! Miseria.

SCHAUNARD
Fra mezz'ora è morta!

MIMÌ
Ho tanto freddo.
Se avessi un manicotto!
Queste mie mani riscaldare
non si potranno mai?

RODOLFO
Qui. Nelle mie, Taci.
Il parlar ti stanca.

MIMÌ
Ho un po' di tosse.
Ci sono avvezza.
Buon giorno, Marcello,
Schaunard, Colline, buon giorno.
Tutti qui, tutti qui
sorridenti a Mimì.

RODOLFO
Beloved lips,
you speak to me again.

MUSETTA
What is there in the house?

MARCELLO
Nothing.

MUSETTA
No coffee? No wine?

MARCELLO
Nothing. Poverty!

SCHAUNARD
She can't last an hour!

MIMÌ
I'm so cold.
If I had a muff!
Won't these hands of mine
ever be warm?

RODOLFO
Here. In mine. Don't speak.
You'll tire yourself.

MIMÌ
It's just a little cough.
I'm used to it.
Hello, Marcello,
Schaunard, Colline…
All of you are here,
smiling at Mimì.

RODOLFO
Non parlar, non parlar.

MIMÌ
Parlo pian. Non temere.
Marcello date retta
è assai buona Musetta.

MARCELLO *(porge la mano a Musetta)*
Lo so. Lo so.

MUSETTA *(dà gli orecchini a Marcello)*
A te, vendi, riporta
qualche cordial.
Manda un dottore!

RODOLFO
Riposa.

MIMÌ
Tu non mi lasci?

RODOLFO
No, no!

MUSETTA
Ascolta!
Forse è l'ultima volta che ha espresso
un desiderio,
poveretta! Pel manicotto
io vo. Con te verrò.

MARCELLO
Sei buona, o mia Musetta.

Marcello and Musetta go out.

RODOLFO
Don't speak, don't…

MIMÌ
I'll speak softly. Don't fear.
Marcello, believe me—
Musetta is so good.

MARCELLO *(holds Musetta's hand)*
I know. I know.

MUSETTA *(gives her earrings to Marcello)*
Here. Sell them. Bring
back some cordial
and send the doctor!

RODOLFO
Rest now!

MIMÌ
You wont leave me?

RODOLFO
No, no!

MUSETTA
Listen!
Perhaps it's the poor thing's
last request.
I'll get the muff.
I'm coming with you.

MARCELLO
How good you are, Musetta.

Vecchia zimarra The philosopher Colline resolves to sell his coat in order to make Mimì comfortable, and he bids the garment farewell in a brief, touching aria. The tenor Enrico Caruso once sang this aria in a Metropolitan Opera performance of La Bohème in Philadelphia. The bass had lost his voice and so—with no other alternative available since the act moves so swiftly that no one onstage would have time to leave and come back—Caruso, who was singing Rodolfo, turned his back to the audience and sang the aria while the bass mimed it.

COLLINE *(levandosi il pastrano)*	**COLLINE** *(taking off his greatcoat)*
Vecchia zimarra, senti,	Listen, my venerable coat,
io resto al pian, tu ascendere	I'm staying behind, you'll
il sacro monte or devi.	go on to greater heights.
Le mie grazie ricevi.	I give you my thanks.
Mai non curvasti il logoro	You never bowed your worn back
dorso ai ricchi ed ai potenti.	to the rich or powerful.
Passar nelle tue tasche	You held in your pockets
come in antri tranquilli	poets and philosophers
filosofi e poeti.	as if in tranquil grottoes…
Ora che i giorni lieti	Now that those happy times
fuggir, ti dico addio,	have fled, I bid you farewell,
fedele amico mio. Addio.	faithful old friend. Farewell.

He puts the bundle under his arm, then whispers to Schaunard.

Schaunard, ognuno per diversa via	Schaunard, each separately,
mettiamo insieme due atti di pietà;	let's combine two kindly acts;
io…questo!…E tu…	mine is this…and you…
lasciali soli là…	leave the two of them alone.

SCHAUNARD	**SCHAUNARD**
Filosofo, ragioni!	Philosopher, you're right!
È ver… Vo via!	I'll go along.

They leave.

DISC NO. 2/TRACK 15

Sono andati? **Alone together at last, while the others run errands to fetch things to relieve Mimì's discomfort, Mimì and Rodolfo recall their happier days in a nostalgic duet that ends with Mimì fainting as she recalls the words Rodolfo sang when he first touched her hand (04:03).**

MIMÌ

Sono andati? Fingevo di dormire
perché volli con te sola restare.
Ho tante cose che ti voglio dire,
o una sola ma grande come il mare,
come il mare profonda ed infinita...
Sei il mio amor...e tutta la mia vita.

MIMÌ

Have they gone? I pretended to sleep
because I wanted to be alone with you.
I've so many things to tell you,
or one thing—huge as the sea,
deep and infinite as the sea...
I love you...you're all my life.

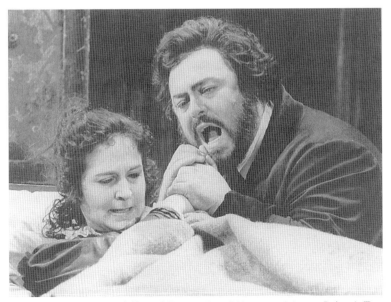

Luciano Pavarotti as Rodolfo and Fiamma Izzo D'Amico as Mimì in Peking's Tian Qiao Theatre's 1986 production of *La Bohème*.

RODOLFO

Ah Mimì, mia bella Mimì!

MIMÌ

Son bella ancora?

RODOLFO

Bella come un'aurora.

MIMÌ

Hai sbagliato il raffronto.
Volevi dir bella
come un tramonto
"Mi chiamano Mimì…
il perché non so"

RODOLFO

Tornò al nido la rondine
e cinguetta.

He takes the bonnet from its place over his heart.

MIMÌ

La mia cuffietta!
La mia cuffietta!
Ah! te lo rammenti
quando sono entrata
la prima volta là?

RODOLFO

Se lo rammento!

MIMÌ

Il lume s'era spento.

RODOLFO

Ah! my beautiful Mimì!

MIMÌ

Am I beautiful still?

RODOLFO

Beautiful as the dawn.

MIMÌ

You've mistaken the image
you should have said,
beautiful as the sunset.
"They call me Mimì…
but I don't know why."

RODOLFO

The swallow comes back to her nest to
twitter.

MIMÌ

My bonnet!
My bonnet!
Ah! do you remember
when I came in here
the first time?

RODOLFO

Do I remember!

MIMÌ

The light had gone out.

RODOLFO

Eri tanto turbata.

Poi smarristi la chiave…

MIMÌ

E a cercarla tastoni ti sei messo!

RODOLFO

E cerca, cerca…

MIMÌ

Mio bel signorino,

posso ben dirlo adesso,

lei la trovò assai presto.

RODOLFO

Aiutavo il destino.

MIMÌ

Era buio e il mio rossor

non si vedeva…

"Che gelida manina…

Se la lasci riscaldar…"

Era buio e la man

tu mi prendevi…

Mimì has another spasm, a fit of choking.

RODOLFO

Oh Dio! Mimì!

Schaunard enters at that moment.

SCHAUNARD

Che avvien?

RODOLFO

You were so upset.

Then you lost your key…

MIMÌ

And you knelt to hunt for it!

RODOLFO

I searched and searched…

MIMÌ

My dear sir,

now I can tell you

you found it quick enough.

RODOLFO

I was helping Fate.

MIMÌ

It was dark. You couldn't

see me blushing.

"How cold your little hand is…

Let me warm it for you…"

It was dark. You took

my hand in yours…

RODOLFO

Good God! Mimì!

SCHAUNARD

What's wrong?

MIMÌ	**MIMÌ**
Nulla. Sto bene.	Nothing. I'm fine.
RODOLFO	**RODOLFO**
Zitta. Per carità.	Please…don't talk.
MIMÌ	**MIMÌ**
Si, si, perdona.	Yes, yes forgive me.
Or sarò buona.	Now I'll be good.

Marcello and Musetta come back, then Colline. Musetta sets a candle on the table.

DISC NO. 2/TRACK 16

Dorme? … Riposa **Matters worsen. Mimì lays dying. Musetta prays for her soul, but Schaunard realizes that Mimì has, in fact, died (03:07). Rodolfo is the last to realize it, and he is at first unwilling to accept it. As Marcello tells him to have courage, the orchestra speaks first, the French horns wailing in sorrow (03:45). As Rodolfo cries Mimì's name, a tragic phrase from her third-act farewell aria brings the opera to an end.**

MUSETTA	**MUSETTA**
Dorme?	Is she sleeping?
RODOLFO	**RODOLFO**
Riposa.	She's resting.
MARCELLO	**MARCELLO**
Ho veduto il dottore.	I saw the doctor.
Verrà. Gli ho fatto fretta.	He's coming. I made him hurry.
Ecco il cordial.	Here's the cordial.
MIMÌ	**MIMÌ**
Chi parla?	Who's speaking?
MUSETTA *(porgendo il manicotto)*	**MUSETTA** *(handing her the muff)*
Io, Musetta.	Me. Musetta.

MIMÌ

O come è bello e morbido!
Non più, non più, le mani
allividite. Il tepore le abbellirà.

to Rodolfo

Sei tu che me lo doni?

MUSETTA

Sì.

MIMÌ

Tu! Spensierato!
Grazie. Ma costerà
Piangi? Sto bene.
Pianger così perché?
Qui…amor…sempre con te!
Le mani…al caldo…e dormire.

Silence

MIMÌ

Oh, how lovely and soft it is.
No more, no more…my hands all
ugly and cold…the warmth will heal them.

Did you give it to me?

MUSETTA

Yes, he did.

MIMÌ

You spendthrift!
Thank you…but the cost…
You're crying? I'm well.
Why are you crying like this?
Here…beloved…with you always!
My hands…the warmth…to sleep.

RODOLFO
Che ha detto il medico?

RODOLFO
What did the doctor say?

MARCELLO
Verrà.

MARCELLO
He's coming.

MUSETTA (*pregando*)
Madonna benedetta,
fate la grazia a questa poveretta
che non debba morire.

MUSETTA (*praying*)
Oh blessed Mother,
be merciful to this poor child
who doesn't deserve to die.

breaking off, to Marcello

Qui ci vuole un riparo
perché la fiamma sventola.

We need a shade here;
the candle's flickering.

Marcello sets a book on the table which acts as a shade.

Così.
E che possa guarire.
Madonna santa, io sono
indegna di perdono,
mentre invece Mimì
è un angelo del cielo.

So.
Let her get well,
Holy Mother, I know
I'm unworthy of forgiveness,
but Mimì is an angel
come down from heaven.

RODOLFO
Io spero ancora. Vi pare
che sia grave?

RODOLFO
I still have hope.
You think it's serious?

MUSETTA
Non credo.

MUSETTA
I don't think so.

Schaunard approaches the bed.

SCHAUNARD (*piano a Marcello*)
Marcello, è spirata.

SCHAUNARD (*softly to Marcello*)
Marcello, she's dead.

COLLINE *(entra e dà del danaro a Musetta)*
Musetta, a voi.
Come va?

COLLINE *(enters, and gives money to Musetta)*
Here, Musetta.
How is she?

RODOLFO
Vedi, è tranquilla.

RODOLFO
You see, she's resting.

Rodolfo becomes aware of the strange expression of the others.

Che vuol dire?
Quell'andare e venire…
Quel guardarmi così?…

What does this mean?
This going back and forth?
Why are you looking at me like this?

MARCELLO
Coraggio.

MARCELLO
Courage.

Rodolfo runs over to the bed.

RODOLFO
Mimì!…Mimì!…

RODOLFO
Mimì!…Mimì!…

THE END

Jim Caldwell/Houston Grand Opera: 117, 153; Corbis-Bettmann: 10, 13, 17, 20, 49, 128; Dover Publications, Inc.: 9, 19, 23, 31; Hans Fahrmeyer/Santa Fe Opera: 38, 55; Winnie Klotz/Metropolitan Opera: 8, 36–37, 41; Joan Marcus: 14; Metropolitan Opera Archives: 18, 39, 42, 44, 45, 47, 80, 86, 107, 130; Ferrucio Nuzzo/EMI Ltd.: 26, 50; Picture Fund coutesy, Museum of Fine Arts, Boston: 32, 53; Dan Rest/Lyric Opera of Chicago: 24–25; Reuters/Corbis-Bettmann: 149; Marty Sohl/San Francisco Opera: 30; Underwood Photo Archives: 11; UPI/Corbis-Bettmann: 82.

LA BOHÈME

Giacomo Puccini

COMPACT DISC ONE

ATTO PRIMO/ACT ONE/ERSTER AKT/PREMIER ACTE

1	Questo Mar Rosso	4:14
2	Pensier profondo!	1:18
	Marcello/Rodolfo/Colline	
3	Legna!…Sigari!	3:41
	Rodolfo/Marcello/Colline/Schaunard	
4	Si può?…Chi è là?	5:09
	Benoit/Marcello/Schaunard/Colline/Rodolfo	
5	Io resto per terminar	0:54
	Rodolfo/Marcello/Colline/Schaunard	
6	Non sono in vena…Scusi	2:24
7	Oh! sventata, sventata!	1:37
	Rodolfo/Mimì	
8	Che gelida manima!	4:27
	Rodolfo	
9	Sì. Mi chiamano Mimì	4:54
	Mimì/Rodolfo	
10	Ehi! Rodolfo!	0:40
	Schaunard/Colline/Marcello/Rodolfo/Mimì	
11	O soave fanciulla	3:57
	Rodolfo/Mimì	